# THE UNSOLVED RIDDLE
## OF SOCIAL JUSTICE

# THE
# UNSOLVED RIDDLE
## OF
# SOCIAL JUSTICE

## BY STEPHEN LEACOCK
B. A., Ph. D., Litt. D., F. R. S. C.

*Professor of Political Economy at McGill University, Montreal*

Author of "Essays and Literary Studies," Etc.

NEW YORK: JOHN LANE COMPANY
LONDON : JOHN LANE, THE BODLEY HEAD
TORONTO: S. B. GUNDY: MCMXX

Copyright, 1920,
By John Lane Company

# CONTENTS

# THE UNSOLVED RIDDLE
## OF SOCIAL JUSTICE

## I.—The Troubled Outlook of the Present Hour

THESE are troubled times. As the echoes of the war die away the sound of a new conflict rises on our ears. All the world is filled with industrial unrest. Strike follows upon strike. A world that has known five years of fighting has lost its taste for the honest drudgery of work. Cincinnatus will not back to his plow, or, at the best, stands sullenly between his plow-handles arguing for a higher wage.

The wheels of industry are threatening to stop. The laborer will not work because the pay is too low and the hours are too long. The producer cannot employ him because the wage is too high, and the hours are too short. If the high wage is paid and the short hours are granted, then the price of the thing made, so it seems, rises higher still. Even the high wages will not buy it. The process apparently moves in a circle with no cessation to it. The increased wages seem only to aggravate the increasing prices. Wages and prices, rising together, call perpetually for more money, or at least more tokens and symbols, more paper credit in the form of checks and deposits, with a value that is no longer based on the rock-bottom of redemption into hard coin, but that floats upon the mere atmosphere of expectation.

But the sheer quantity of the inflated currency and false money forces prices higher still. The familiar landmarks of wages, salaries and prices are being obliterated. The "scrap of paper" with which the war began stays with us as its legacy. It lies upon the industrial landscape like snow, covering up, as best it may, the bare poverty of a world desolated by war.

Under such circumstances national finance seems turned into a delirium. Billions are voted where once a few poor millions were thought extravagant. The war debts of the Allied Nations, not yet fully computed, will run from twenty-five to forty billion dollars apiece. But the debts of the governments appear on the other side of the ledger as the assets of the citizens. What is the meaning of it? Is it wealth or is it poverty? The world seems filled with money and short of goods, while even in this very scarcity a new luxury has broken out. The capitalist rides in his ten thousand dollar motor car. The seven-dollar-a-day artisan plays merrily on his gramophone in the broad daylight of his afternoon that is saved, like all else, by being "borrowed" from the morning. He calls the capitalist a "profiteer." The capitalist retorts with calling him a "Bolshevik."

Worse portents appear. Over the rim of the Russian horizon are seen the fierce eyes and the unshorn face of the real and undoubted Bolshevik, waving his red flag. Vast areas of what was a fertile populated world are overwhelmed in chaos. Over Russia there lies a great darkness, spreading ominously westward into Central Europe.   The criminal sits among his corpses.   He feeds upon the wreck of a civilization that was.

The infection spreads.   All over the world the just claims of organized labor are inter-mingled with the underground conspiracy of social revolution.   The public mind is con-fused.   Something approaching to a social panic appears.   To some minds the demand for law and order overwhelms all other thoughts.   To others the fierce desire for so-cial justice obliterates all fear of a general catastrophe.   They push nearer and nearer to the brink of the abyss.   The warning cry of "back" is challenged by the eager shout of "forward!"   The older methods of social progress are abandoned as too slow.   The older weapons of social defense are thrown aside as too blunt.   Parliamentary discussion is powerless.   It limps in the wake of the pop-ular movement.   The "state", as we knew it, threatens to dissolve into labor unions, con-ventions, boards of conciliation, and confer-ences.   Society shaken to its base, hurls itself into the industrial suicide of the general strike, refusing to feed itself, denying its own wants.

This is a time such as there never was before. It represents a vast social transformation in which there is at stake, and may be lost, all that has been gained in the slow centuries of material progress and in which there may be achieved some part of all that has been dreamed in the age-long passion for social justice.

For the time being, the constituted governments of the world survive as best they may and accomplish such things as they can, planless, or planning at best only for the day. Sufficient, and more than sufficient, for the day is the evil thereof.

Never then was there a moment in which there was greater need for sane and serious thought. It is necessary to consider from the ground up the social organization in which we live and the means whereby it may be altered and expanded to meet the needs of the time to come. We must do this or perish. If we do not mend the machine, there are forces

moving in the world that will break it. The
blind Samson of labor will seize upon the pil-
lars of society and bring them down in a common destruction.

.    .    .    .    .

Few persons can attain to adult life without
being profoundly impressed by the appalling
inequalities of our human lot. Riches and
poverty jostle one another upon our streets.
The tattered outcast dozes on his bench while
the chariot of the wealthy is drawn by. The
palace is the neighbor of the slum. We are,
in modern life, so used to this that we no
longer see it.

Inequality begins from the very cradle.
Some are born into an easy and sheltered af-
fluence. Others are the children of mean and
sordid want. For some the long toil of life
begins in the very bloom time of childhood
and ends only when the broken and exhausted
body sinks into a penurious old age. For
others life is but a foolish leisure with mock
activities and mimic avocations to mask its use-
lessness. And as the circumstances vary so

too does the native endowment of the body and the mind. Some born in poverty rise to wealth. An inborn energy and capacity bid defiance to the ill-will of fate. Others sink. The careless hand lets fall the cradle gift of wealth.

Thus all about us is the moving and shifting spectacle of riches and poverty, side by side, inextricable.

The human mind, lost in a maze of inequalities that it cannot explain and evils that it cannot, singly, remedy, must adapt itself as best it can. An acquired indifference to the ills of others is the price at which we live. A certain dole of sympathy, a casual mite of personal relief is the mere drop that any one of us alone can cast into the vast ocean of human misery. Beyond that we must harden ourselves lest we too perish. We feed well while others starve. We make fast the doors of our lighted houses against the indigent and the hungry. What else can we do? If we shelter *one* what is that? And if we try to shelter all, we are ourselves shelterless.

But the contrast thus presented is one that has acquired a new meaning in the age in which we live. The poverty of earlier days was the outcome of the insufficiency of human labor to meet the primal needs of human kind. It is not so now. We live in an age that is at best about a century and a half old—the age of machinery and power. Our common reading of history has obscured this fact. Its pages are filled with the purple gowns of kings and the scarlet trappings of the warrior. Its record is largely that of battles and sieges, of the brave adventure of discovery and the vexed slaughter of the nations. It has long since dismissed as too short and simple for its pages, the short and simple annals of the poor. And the record is right enough. Of the poor what is there to say? They were born; they lived; they died. They followed their leaders, and their names are forgotten.

But written thus our history has obscured the greatest fact that ever came into it—the colossal change that separates our little era of a century and a half from all the preceding history of mankind—separates it so completely that a great gulf lies between, across which comparison can scarcely pass, and on the other side of which a new world begins.

It has been the custom of our history to use the phrase the "new world" to mark the discoveries of Columbus and the treasure-hunt of a Cortes or a Pizarro. But what of that? The America that they annexed to Europe was merely a new domain added to a world already old. The "new world" was really found in the wonder-years of the eighteenth and early nineteenth centuries. Mankind really entered upon it when the sudden progress of liberated science bound the fierce energy of expanding stream and drew the eager lightning from the cloud.

Here began indeed, in the drab surroundings of the workshop, in the silent mystery of the laboratory, the magic of the new age.

But we do not commonly realize the vastness of the change. Much of our life and much of our thought still belongs to the old world. Our education is still largely framed on the old

pattern.   And our views of poverty and social
betterment, or what is possible and what is not,
are still largely conditioned by it.

In the old world, poverty seemed, and poverty was, the natural and inevitable lot of the
greater portion of mankind.   It was difficult,
with the mean appliances of the time, to wring
subsistence from the reluctant earth.   For the
simplest necessaries and comforts of life all,
or nearly all, must work hard.   Many must
perish for want of them.   Poverty was inevitable and perpetual.   The poor must look to
the brightness of a future world for the con-
solation that they were denied in this.   Seen
thus poverty became rather a blessing than
a curse, or at least a dispensation prescribing
the proper lot of man.   Life itself was but a
preparation and a trial—a threshing floor
where, under the "tribulation" of want, the
wheat was beaten from the straw.   Of this
older view much still survives, and much that is
ennobling.   Nor is there any need to say good-
by to it.   Even if poverty were gone, the flail

could still beat hard enough upon the grain and chaff of humanity.

But turn to consider the magnitude of the change that has come about with the era of machinery and the indescribable increase which it has brought to man's power over his environment. There is no need to recite here in detail the marvelous record of mechanical progress that constituted the "industrial revolution" of the eighteenth century. The utilization of coal for the smelting of iron ore; the invention of machinery that could spin and weave; the application of the undreamed energy of steam as a motive force, the building of canals and the making of stone roads—these proved but the beginnings. Each stage of invention called for a further advance. The quickening of one part of the process necessitated the "speeding up" of all the others. It placed a premium— a reward already in sight—upon the next advance. Mechanical spinning called forth the power loom. The increase in production called for new means of transport. The improvement of transport still further swelled the volume of production. The steamboat of 1809 and the steam locomotive of 1830 were the direct result of what had gone before. Most important of all, the movement had become a conscious one. Invention was no longer the fortuitous result of a happy chance. Mechanical progress, the continual increase of power and the continual surplus of product became an essential part of the environment, and an unconscious element in the thought and outlook of the civilized world.

No wonder that the first aspect of the age of machinery was one of triumph. Man had vanquished nature. The elemental forces of wind and fire, of rushing water and driving storm before which the savage had cowered low for shelter, these had become his servants. The forest that had blocked his path became his field. The desert blossomed as his garden.

The aspect of industrial life altered. The domestic industry of the cottage and the individual labor of the artisan gave place to the factory with its regiment of workers and its

steam-driven machinery. The economic isola-
tion of the single worker, of the village, even
of the district and the nation, was lost in the
general cohesion in which the whole industrial
world merged into one.

The life of the individual changed accord-
ingly. In the old world his little sphere was
allotted to him and there he stayed. His village was his horizon. The son of the weaver
wove and the smith reared his children to his
trade. Each did his duty, or was adjured to
do it, in the "state of life to which it had
pleased God to call him." Migration to distant occupations or to foreign lands was but for
the adventurous few. The ne'er-do-well blew,
like seed before the wind, to distant places, but
mankind at large stayed at home. Here and
there exceptional industry or extraordinary capacity raised the artisan to wealth and turned
the "man" into the "master." But for the
most part even industry and endowment were
powerless against the inertia of custom and the
dead-weight of environment. The universal
ignorance of the working class broke down the

aspiring force of genius. Mute inglorious
Miltons were buried in country churchyards.

In the new world all this changed. The individual became but a shifting atom in the vast
complex, moving from place to place, from occupation to occupation and from gradation to
gradation of material fortune.

The process went further and further. The
machine penetrated everywhere, thrusting aside
with its gigantic arm the feeble efforts of handi-
craft. It laid its hold upon agriculture, sow-
ing and reaping the grain and transporting it
to the ends of the earth. Then as the nineteenth century drew towards its close, even the
age of steam power was made commonplace
by achievements of the era of electricity.

All this is familiar enough. The record of
the age of machinery is known to all. But the
strange mystery, the secret that lies concealed
within its organization, is realized by but few.
It offers, to those who see it aright, the most
perplexing industrial paradox ever presented in
the history of mankind. With all our wealth,
we are still poor. After a century and a half

of labor-saving machinery, we work about
as hard as ever. With a power over nature multiplied a hundred fold, nature still
conquers us. And more than this. There
are many senses in which the machine age
seems to leave the great bulk of civilized humanity, the working part of it, worse off in-
stead of better. The nature of our work has
changed. No man now makes anything. He
makes only a part of something, feeding and
tending a machine that moves with relentless
monotony in the routine of which both the
machine and its tender are only a fractional
part.

For the great majority of the workers, the
interest of work as such is gone. It is a task
done consciously for a wage, one eye upon the
clock. The brave independence of the keeper
of the little shop contrasts favorably with the
mock dignity of a floor walker in an "establish-
ment." The varied craftsmanship of the artisan had in it something of the creative element
that was the parent motive of sustained industry. The dull routine of the factory hand in

a cotton mill has gone.    The life of a pioneer settler in America two hundred years ago, penurious and dangerous as it was, stands out brightly beside the dull and meaningless toil of his descendant.

The picture must not be drawn in colors too sinister.    In the dullest work and in the meanest lives in the new world to-day there are elements that were lacking in the work of the old world.    The universal spread of elementary education, the universal access to the printed page, and the universal hope of better things, if not for oneself, at least for one's children, and even the universal restlessness that the industrialism of to-day have brought are better things than the dull plodding passivity of the older world.    Only a false mediævalism can paint the past in colors superior to the present. The haze of distance that dims the mountains with purple, shifts also the crude colors of the past into the soft glory of retrospect.    Misled by these, the sentimentalist may often sigh for an age that in a nearer view would be seen filled with cruelty and suffering.    But even when we have made every allowance for the all too human tendency to soften down the past, it remains true that in many senses the processes of industry for the worker have lost in attractiveness and power of absorption of the mind during the very period when they have gained so enormously in effectiveness and in power of production.

The essential contrast lies between the vastly increased power of production and its apparent inability to satisfy for all humanity the most elementary human wants; between the immeasurable saving of labor effected by machinery and the brute fact of the continuance of hard-driven, unceasing toil.

Of the extent of this increased power of production we can only speak in general terms. No one, as far as I am aware, has yet essayed to measure it. Nor have we any form of calculus or computation that can easily be applied. If we wish to compare the gross total of production effected to-day with that accomplished a hundred and fifty years ago, the means, the basis of calculation, is lacking. Vast numbers

of the things produced now were not then in
existence. A great part of our production of
to-day culminates not in productive goods, but
in services, as in forms of motion, or in ability
to talk across a distance.

It is true that statistics that deal with the
world's production of cotton, or of oil, or of
iron and steel present stupendous results. But
even these do not go far enough. For the
basic raw materials are worked into finer and
finer forms to supply new "wants" as they are
called, and to represent a vast quantity of "sat-
isfactions" not existing before.

Nor is the money calculus of any avail.
Comparison by prices breaks down entirely. A
bushel of wheat stands about where it stood
before and could be calculated. But the computation, let us say, in price-values of the Sunday newspapers produced in one week in New
York or the annual output of photographic apparatus, would defy comparison. Of the enormous increase in the gross total of human goods
there is no doubt. We have only to look about
us to see it. The endless miles of railways,

the vast apparatus of the factories, the soaring structures of the cities bear easy witness to it. Yet it would be difficult indeed to compute by what factor the effectiveness of human labor working with machinery has been increased.

But suppose we say, since one figure is as good as another, that it has been increased a hundred times. This calculation must be well within the facts and can be used as merely a more concrete way of saying that the power of production has been vastly increased. During the period of this increase, the numbers of mankind in the industrial countries have perhaps been multiplied by three to one. This again is inexact, since there are no precise figures of population that cover the period. But all that is meant is that the increase in one case is, quite obviously, colossal, and in the other case is evidently not very much.

Here then is the paradox.

If the ability to produce goods to meet human wants has multiplied so that each man accomplishes almost thirty or forty times what he did before, then the world at large ought to be about thirty or fifty times better off.    But it is not.    Or else, as the other possible alternative, the working hours of the world should have been cut down to about one in thirty of what they were before.    But they are not. How, then, are we to explain this extraordinary discrepancy between human power and resulting human happiness?

The more we look at our mechanism of production the more perplexing it seems.    Suppose an observer were to look down from the cold distance of the moon upon the seething ant-hill of human labor presented on the surface of our globe; and suppose that such an observer knew nothing of our system of individual property, of money payments and wages and contracts, but viewed our labor as merely that of a mass of animated beings trying to supply their wants. The spectacle to his eyes would be strange indeed.    Mankind viewed in the mass would be seen to produce a certain amount of absolutely necessary things, such as food, and then to stop.    In spite of the fact that there was not food enough to go round, and that large numbers must die of starvation or perish slowly from under-nutrition, the production of food would stop at some point a good deal short of universal satisfaction. So, too, with the production of clothing, shelter and other necessary things; never enough would seem to be produced, and this apparently not by accident or miscalculation, but as if some peculiar social law were at work adjusting production to the point where there is just not enough, and leaving it there. The countless millions of workers would be seen to turn their untired energies and their all-powerful machinery away from the production of necessary things to the making of mere comforts; and from these, again, while still stopping short of a general satisfaction, to the making of luxuries and superfluities. The wheels would never stop. The activity would never tire. Mankind, mad with the energy of activity, would be seen to pursue the fleeing phantom of insatiable desire. Thus among the huge mass of accumulated commodities the simplest wants would go unsatisfied. Half-fed men would dig for diamonds, and men shel-

tered by a crazy roof erect the marble walls
of palaces. The observer might well remain
perplexed at the pathetic discord between human work and human wants. Something, he
would feel assured, must be at fault either with
the social instincts of man or with the social
order under which he lives.

And herein lies the supreme problem that
faces us in this opening century. The period
of five years of war has shown it to us in a
clearer light than fifty years of peace. War
is destruction—the annihilation of human life,
the destruction of things made with generations
of labor, the misdirection of productive power
from making what is useful to making what
is useless. In the great war just over, some
seven million lives were sacrificed; eight million
tons of shipping were sunk beneath the sea;
some fifty million adult males were drawn from
productive labor to the lines of battle; behind
them uncounted millions labored day and night
at making the weapons of destruction. One
might well have thought that such a gigantic
misdirection of human energy would have

brought the industrial world to a standstill within a year. So people did think. So thought a great number, perhaps the greater number, of the financiers and economists and industrial leaders trained in the world in which we used to live. The expectation was unfounded. Great as is the destruction of war, not even five years of it have broken the productive machine. And the reason is now plain enough. Peace, also—or peace under the old conditions of industry—is infinitely wasteful of human energy. Not more than one adult worker in ten—so a leading American economist has declared—is employed on necessary things. The other nine perform superfluous services. War turns them from making the glittering superfluities of peace to making its grim engines of destruction. But while the tenth man still labors, the machine, though creaking with its dislocation, can still go on. The economics of war, therefore, has thrown its lurid light upon the economics of peace.

These I propose in the succeeding chapters to examine. But it might be well before doing so to lay stress upon the fact that while admitting all the shortcomings and the injustices of the régime under which we have lived, I am not one of those who are able to see a short and single remedy. Many people when presented with the argument above, would settle it at once with the word "socialism." Here, they say, is the immediate and natural remedy. I confess at the outset, and shall develop later, that I cannot view it so. Socialism is a mere beautiful dream, possible only for the angels. The attempt to establish it would hurl us over the abyss. Our present lot is sad, but the frying pan is at least better than the fire.

## II.—*Life, Liberty and the Pursuit of Happiness*

"ALL men," wrote Thomas Jefferson in framing the Declaration of Independence, "have an inalienable right to life, liberty and the pursuit of happiness." The words are more than a felicitous phrase. They express even more than the creed of a nation. They embody in themselves the uppermost thought of the era that was dawning when they were written. They stand for the same view of society which, in that very year of 1776, Adam Smith put before the world in his immortal "Wealth of Nations" as the "System of Natural Liberty." In this system mankind placed its hopes for over half a century and under it the industrial civilization of the age of machinery rose to the plenitude of its power.

In the preceding chapter an examination has been made of the purely mechanical side of the era of machine production. It has been shown that the age of machinery has been in a certain sense one of triumph, of the triumphant conquest of nature, but in another sense one of perplexing failure. The new forces controlled by mankind have been powerless as yet to remove want and destitution, hard work and social discontent. In the midst of accumulated wealth social justice seems as far away as ever.

It remains now to discuss the intellectual development of the modern age of machinery and the way in which it has moulded the thoughts and the outlook of mankind.

Few men think for themselves. The thoughts of most of us are little more than imitations and adaptations of the ideas of stronger minds. The influence of environment conditions, if it does not control, the mind of man. So it comes about that every age or generation has its dominant and uppermost thoughts, its peculiar way of looking at things and its peculiar basis of opinion on which its collective action and its social regulations rest. All this is largely unconscious. The average citizen of three generations ago was probably not aware that he was an extreme individualist. The average citizen of to-day is not conscious of the fact that he has ceased to be one. The man of three generations ago had certain ideas which he held to be axiomatic, such as that his house was his castle, and that property was property and that what was his was his. But these were to him things so obvious that he could not conceive any reasonable person doubting them. So, too, with the man of to-day. He has come to believe in such things as old age pensions and national insurance. He submits to bachelor taxes and he pays for the education of other people's children; he speculates much on the limits of inheritance, and he even meditates profound alterations in the right of property in land. His house is no longer his castle. He has taken down its fences, and "boulevarded" its grounds till it merges into those of his neighbors. Indeed he probably does not live in a house at all, but in a mere "apartment" or subdivision of a house which he shares with a multiplicity of people. Nor does he any longer draw water from his own well or go to bed by the light of his own candle: for such services as these his life is so mixed up with "franchises" and "public utilities" and other things unheard of by his own great-grandfather, that it is hopelessly intertangled with that of his fellow citizens. In fine, there is little left but his own conscience into which he can withdraw.

Such a man is well aware that times have changed since his great-grandfather's day. But he is not aware of the profound extent to which his own opinions have been affected by the changing times. He is no longer an individualist. He has become by brute force of circumstances a sort of collectivist, puzzled only as to how much of a collectivist to be.

Individualism of the extreme type is, therefore, long since out of date. To attack it is merely to kick a dead dog. But the essential problem of to-day is to know how far we are to depart from its principles. There are those

who tell us—and they number many millions—
that we must abandon them entirely. Industrial society, they say, must be reorganized
from top to bottom; private industry must
cease. All must work for the state; only in a
socialist commonwealth can social justice be
found. There are others, of whom the present writer is one, who see in such a programme
nothing but disaster: yet who consider that the
individualist principle of "every man for himself" while it makes for national wealth and
accumulated power, favors overmuch the few
at the expense of the many, puts an over-great
premium upon capacity, assigns too harsh a
punishment for easy indolence, and, what is
worse, exposes the individual human being too
cruelly to the mere accidents of birth and fortune. Under such a system, in short, to those
who have is given and from those who have not
is taken away even that which they have.
There are others again who still view individualism just as the vast majority of our great-
grandfathers viewed it, as a system hard but
just: as awarding to every man the fruit of his

own labor and the punishment of his own idleness, and as visiting, in accordance with the
stern but necessary ordination of our existence,
the sins of the father upon the child.

The proper starting point, then, for all discussion of the social problem is the considera-
tion of the individualist theory of industrial
society.   This grew up, as all the world knows,
along with the era of machinery itself.   It had
its counterpart on the political side in the
rise of representative democratic government.
Machinery, industrial liberty, political democracy—these three things represent the basis of
the progress of the nineteenth century.

The chief exposition of the system is found
in the work of the classical economists—Adam
Smith and his followers of half a century—who
created the modern science of political economy.   Beginning as controversialists anxious to
overset a particular system of trade regulation,
they ended by becoming the exponents of a new
social order.   Modified and amended as their
system is in its practical application, it still

largely conditions our outlook to-day. It is to this system that we must turn.

The general outline of the classical theory of political economy is so clear and so simple that it can be presented within the briefest compass. It began with certain postulates, or assumptions, to a great extent unconscious, of the conditions to which it applied. It assumed the existence of the state and of contract. It took for granted the existence of individual property, in consumption goods, in capital goods, and, with a certain hesitation, in land. The last assumption was not perhaps without misgivings: Adam Smith was disposed to look askance at landlords as men who gathered where they had not sown. John Stuart Mill, as is well known, was more and more inclined, with advancing reflection, to question the sanctity of landed property as the basis of social institutions. But for the most part property, contract and the coercive state were fundamental assumptions with the classicists.

With this there went, on the psychological

side, the further assumption of a general selfishness or self-seeking as the principal motive
of the individual in the economic sphere.
Oddly enough this assumption—the most war-
rantable of the lot—was the earliest to fall under disrepute.   The plain assertion that every
man looks out for himself (or at best for himself and his immediate family) touches the tender conscience of humanity.   It is an unpala-
table truth.   None the less it is the most nearly
true of all the broad generalizations that can
be attempted in regard to mankind.

The essential problem then of the classicists
was to ask what would happen if an industrial
community, possessed of the modern control
over machinery and power, were allowed to follow the promptings of "enlightened selfishness"
in an environment based upon free contract and
the right of property in land and goods.   The
answer was of the most cheering description.
The result would be a progressive amelioration
of society, increasing in proportion to the com-
pleteness with which the fundamental principles
involved were allowed to act, and tending ulti-

mately towards something like a social millennium or perfection of human society. One easily recalls the almost reverent attitude of Adam Smith towards this system of industrial liberty which he exalted into a kind of natural theology: and the way in which Mill, a deist but not a Christian, was able to fit the whole apparatus of individual liberty into its place in an ordered universe. The world "runs of itself," said the economist. We have only to leave it alone. And the maxim of *laissez faire* became the last word of social wisdom.

The argument of the classicists ran thus. If there is everywhere complete economic freedom, then there will ensue in consequence a régime of social justice. If every man is allowed to buy and sell goods, labor and property, just as suits his own interest, then the prices and wages that result are either in the exact measure of social justice or, at least, are perpetually moving towards it. The price of any commodity at any moment is, it is true, a "market price," the resultant of the demand and the supply; but behind this operates continually the inexorable law of the cost of production. Sooner or later every price must represent the actual cost of producing the commodity concerned, or, at least, must oscillate now above and now below that point which it is always endeavoring to meet. For if temporary circumstances force the price well above the cost of producing the article in question, then the large profits to be made induce a greater and greater production. The increased volume of the supply thus produced inevitably forces down the price till it sinks to the point of cost. If circumstances (such, for example, as miscalculation and an over-great supply) depress the price below the point of cost, then the discouragement of further production presently shortens the supply and brings the price up again. Price is thus like an oscillating pendulum seeking its point of rest, or like the waves of the sea rising and falling about its level. By this same mechanism the quantity and direction of production, argued the economists, respond automatically to the needs of humanity, or, at least, to the "effec-

tive demand," which the classicist mistook for
the same thing. Just as much wheat or bricks
or diamonds would be produced as the world
called for; to produce too much of any one
thing was to violate a natural law; the falling
price and the resulting temporary loss sternly
rebuked the producer.

In the same way the technical form and
mechanism of production were presumed to respond to an automatic stimulus. Inventions
and improved processes met their own reward.
Labor, so it was argued, was perpetually being saved by the constant introduction of new
uses of machinery.

By a parity of reasoning, the shares received
by all the participants and claimants in the
general process of production were seen to
be regulated in accordance with natural law.
Interest on capital was treated merely as a
particular case under the general theory of
price. It was the purchase price needed to
call forth the "saving" (a form, so to speak,
of production) which brought the capital into
the market. The "profits" of the employer

represented the necessary price paid by society for his services, just enough and not more than enough to keep him and his fellows in operative activity, and always tending under the happy operation of competition to fall to the minimum consistent with social progress.

Rent, the share of the land-owner, offered to the classicist a rather peculiar case. There was here a physical basis of surplus over cost. But, granted the operation of the factors and forces concerned, rent emerged as a differential payment to the fortunate owner of the soil. It did not in any way affect prices or wages, which were rendered neither greater nor less thereby. The full implication of the rent doctrine and its relation to social justice remained obscured to the eye of the classical economist; the fixed conviction that what a man owns is his own created a mist through which the light could not pass.

Wages, finally, were but a further case of value. There was a demand for labor, represented by the capital waiting to remunerate it, and a supply of labor represented by the

existing and increasing working class. Hence
wages, like all other shares and factors, cor-
responded, so it was argued, to social justice.
Whether wages were high or low, whether
hours were long or short, at least the laborer
like everybody else "got what was coming to
him." All possibility of a general increase of
wages depended on the relation of available
capital to the numbers of the working men.

Thus the system as applied to society at
large could be summed up in the consoling
doctrine that every man got what he was worth,
and was worth what he got; that industry and
energy brought their own reward; that national
wealth and individual welfare were one and
the same; that all that was needed for social
progress was hard work, more machinery, more
saving of labor and a prudent limitation of
the numbers of the population.

The application of such a system to legislation and public policy was obvious. It carried with it the principle of *laissez-faire*. The
doctrine of international free trade, albeit the
most conspicuous of its applications, was but

one case under the general law. It taught that the mere organization of labor was powerless to raise wages; that strikes were of no avail, or could at best put a shilling into the pocket of one artisan by taking it out of that of another; that wages and prices could not be regulated by law; that poverty was to a large extent a biological phenomenon representing the fierce struggle of germinating life against the environment that throttles part of it. The poor were like the fringe of grass that fades or dies where it meets the sand of the desert. There could be no social remedy for poverty except the almost impossible remedy of the limitation of life itself. Failing this the economist could wash his hands of the poor.

These are the days of relative judgments and the classical economy, like all else, must be viewed in the light of time and circumstance. With all its fallacies, or rather its shortcomings, it served a magnificent purpose. It opened a road never before trodden from social slavery towards social freedom, from the mediæval autocratic régime of fixed caste and hereditary status towards a régime of equal social justice. In this sense the classical economy was but the fruition, or rather represented the final consciousness of a process that had been going on for centuries, since the breakdown of feudalism and the emancipation of the serf. True, the goal has not been reached. The vision of the universal happiness seen by the economists has proved a mirage. The end of the road is not in sight. But it cannot be doubted that in the long pilgrimage of mankind towards social betterment the economists guided us in the right turning. If we turn again in a new direction, it will at any rate not be in the direction of a return to autocratic mediævalism.

But when all is said in favor of its historic usefulness, the failures and the fallacies of natural liberty have now become so manifest that the system is destined in the coming era to be revised from top to bottom. It is to these failures and fallacies that attention will be drawn in the next chapter.

## III.—The Failures and Fallacies of Natural Liberty

THE rewards and punishments of the economic world are singularly unequal. One man earns as much in a week or even in a day as another does in a year. This man by hard, manual labor makes only enough to pay for humble shelter and plain food. This other by what seems a congenial activity, fascinating as a game of chess, acquires uncounted millions. A third stands idle in the market place asking in vain for work. A fourth lives upon rent, dozing in his chair, and neither toils nor spins. A fifth by the sheer hazard of a lucky "deal" acquires a fortune without work at all. A sixth, scorning to work, earns nothing and gets nothing; in him survives a primitive dislike of labor not yet fully "evoluted out;" he slips through the meshes of civilization to become a "tramp," cadges his food where he can, suns his tattered rags when it is warm and shivers when it is cold, migrating with the birds and reappearing with the flowers of spring.

Yet all are free. This is the distinguishing mark of them as children of our era. They may work or stop. There is no compulsion from without. No man is a slave. Each has his "natural liberty," and each in his degree, great or small, receives his allotted reward.

But is the allotment correct and the reward proportioned by his efforts? Is it fair or unfair, and does it stand for the true measure of social justice?

This is the profound problem of the twentieth century.

The economists and the leading thinkers of the nineteenth century were in no doubt about this question. It was their firm conviction that the system under which we live was, in its broad outline, a system of even justice. They held it true that every man under free competition and individual liberty is awarded just what he is

worth and is worth exactly what he gets: that
the reason why a plain laborer is paid only two
or three dollars a day is because he only "produces" two or three dollars a day: and that
why a skilled engineer is paid ten times as much
is because he "produces" ten times as much.
His work is "worth" ten times that of the plain
laborer. By the same reasoning the salary of
a corporation president who receives fifty thousand dollars a year merely reflects the fact that
the man produces—earns—brings in to the corporation that amount or even more. The big
salary corresponds to the big efficiency.

And there is much in the common experience
of life and the common conduct of business that
seems to support this view. It is undoubtedly
true if we look at any little portion of business activity taken as a fragment by itself. On
the most purely selfish grounds I may find that
it "pays" to hire an expert at a hundred dollars a day, and might find that it spelled ruin
to attempt to raise the wages of my workingmen beyond four dollars a day. Everybody
knows that in any particular business at any

particular place and time with prices at any particular point, there is a wage that can be paid and a wage that can not. And everybody, or nearly everybody, bases on these obvious facts a series of entirely erroneous conclusions. Because we cannot change the part we are apt to think we cannot change the whole. Because one brick in the wall is immovable, we forget that the wall itself might be rebuilt.

The single employer rightly knows that there is a wage higher than he can pay and hours shorter than he can grant. But are the limits that frame him in, real and necessary limits, resulting from the very nature of things, or are they mere products of particular circumstances? This, as a piece of pure economics, does not interest the individual employer a particle. It belongs in the same category as the question of the immortality of the soul and other profundities that have nothing to do with business. But to society at large the question is of an infinite importance.

Now the older economists taught, and the educated world for about a century believed, that these limitations which hedged the particular employer about were fixed and assigned by natural economic law. They represented, as has been explained, the operation of the system of natural liberty by which every man got what he is worth. And it is quite true that the particular employer can no more break away from these limits than he can jump out of his own skin. He can only violate them at the expense of ceasing to be an economic being at all and degenerating into a philanthropist.

But consider for a moment the peculiar nature of the limitations themselves. Every man's limit of what he can pay and what he can take, of how much he can offer and how much he will 'receive, is based on the similar limitations of other people. They are reciprocal to one another. Why should one factory owner not pay ten dollars a day to his hands? Because the others don't. But suppose they all do? Then the output could not be sold at the present price. But why not sell the produce at a higher price? Because at a higher price the consumer can't afford to buy it. But suppose that the consumer, for the things which he himself makes and sells, or for the work which he performs, receives more? What then? The whole thing begins to have a jig-saw look, like a child's toy rack with wooden soldiers on it, expanding and contracting. One searches in vain for the basis on which the relationship rests. And at the end of the analysis one finds nothing but a mere anarchical play of forces, nothing but a give-and-take resting on relative bargaining strength. Every man gets what he can and gives what he has to.

Observe that this is not in the slightest the conclusion of the orthodox economists. Every man, they said, gets what he actually makes, or, by exchange, those things which exactly correspond to it as regards the cost of making them—which have, to use the key-word of the theory, the same value. Let us take a very simple example. If I go fishing with a net which I have myself constructed out of fibers and sticks, and if I catch a fish and if I then roast the fish over a fire which I have made without so much as the intervention of a lucifer

match, then it is I and I alone who have "produced" the roast fish. That is plain enough.
But what if I catch the fish by using a hired
boat and a hired net, or by buying worms as
bait from some one who has dug them? Or
what if I do not fish at all, but get my roast
fish by paying for it a part of the wages I receive for working in a saw mill? Here are a
new set of relationships. How much of the
fish is "produced" by each of the people concerned? And what part of my wages ought I
to pay in return for the part of the fish that
I buy?

Here opens up, very evidently, a perfect
labyrinth of complexity. But it was the labyrinth for which the earlier economist held, so
he thought, the thread. No matter how dark
the passage, he still clung tight to it. And his
thread was his "fundamental equation of value"
whereby each thing and everything is sold (or
tends to be sold) under free competition for
exactly its cost of production. There it was;
as simple as A. B. C.; making the cost of everything proportional to the cost of everything

else, and in itself natural and just; explaining and justifying the variations of wages and salaries on what seems a stern basis of fact. Here is your selling price as a starting point. Given that, you can see at once the reason for the wages paid and the full measure of the payment. To pay more is impossible. To pay less is to invite a competition that will force the payment of more. Or take, if you like, the wages as the starting point: there you are again, —simplicity itself: the selling price will exactly and nicely correspond to cost. True, a part of the cost concerned will be represented not by wages, but by cost of materials; but these, on analysis, dissolve into past wages. Hence the whole process and its explanation revolves around this simple fundamental equation that selling value equals the cost of production.

This was the central part of the economic structure. It was the keystone of the arch. If it holds, all holds. Knock it out and the whole edifice falls into fragments.

A technical student of the schools would digress here, to the great confusion of the reader,

into a discussion of the controversy in the economic cloister between the rival schools of economists as to whether cost governs value or
value governs cost.  The point needs no discussion here, but just such fleeting passing men-
tion as may indicate that the writer is well and
wearily conversant with it.

The fundamental equation of the economist,
then, is that the value of everything is proportionate to its cost.  It requires no little hardi-
hood to say that this proposition is a fallacy.
It lays one open at once, most illogically, to the
charge of being a socialist.  In sober truth it
might as well lay one open to the charge of
being an ornithologist.  I will not, therefore,
say that the proposition that the value of everything equals the cost of production is false.  I
will say that it is *true;* in fact, that is just as true
as that two and two make four: exactly as true
as that, but let it be noted most profoundly,
*only as true as that.*  In other words, it is a
truism, mere equation in terms, telling nothing
whatever.  When I say that two and two make
four I find, after deep thought, that I have

really said *nothing,* or nothing that was not already said at the moment I defined two and defined four.   The new statement that two and two make four adds nothing.   So with the majestic equation of the cost of production.   It means, as far as social application goes, as far as any moral significance or bearing on social reform and the social outlook goes, *absolutely nothing.*   It is not in itself fallacious; how could it be?   But all the social inferences drawn from it are absolute, complete and malicious fallacies.

Any socialist who says this, is quite right. Where he goes wrong is when he tries to build up as truth a set of inferences more fallacious and more malicious still.

But the central economic doctrine of cost can not be shaken by mere denunciation.   Let us examine it and see what is the matter with it. We restate the equation.

*Under perfectly free competition the value or selling price of everything equals, or is perpetually tending to equal, the cost of its production.*   This is the proposition itself, and the inferences derived from it are that there is a "natural price" of everything, and that all "natural prices" are proportionate to cost and to one another; that all wages, apart from temporary fluctuations, are derived from, and limited by, the natural prices paid for the things made: that all payments for the use of capital (interest) are similarly derived and similarly limited; and that consequently the whole economic arrangement, by giving to each person exactly and precisely the fruit of his own labor, conforms exactly to social justice.

Now the trouble with the main proposition just quoted is that each side of the equation is used as the measure of the other. In order to show what natural price is, we add up all the wages that have been paid, and declare that to be the cost and then say that the cost governs the price. Then if we are asked why are wages what they are, we turn the argument backward and say that since the selling price is so and so the wages that can be paid out of it only amount to such and such. This explains nothing. It is a mere argument in a circle. It is as if one tried to explain why one blade of a pair of scissors is four inches long by saying that it has to be the same length as the other. This is quite true of either blade if one takes the length of the other for granted, but as applied to the explanation of the length of the scissors it is worse than meaningless.

This reasoning may seem to many persons mere casuistry, mere sophistical juggling with words. After all, they say, there is such a thing as relative cost, relative difficulty of making things, a difference which rests upon a physical basis. To make one thing requires a lot of labor and trouble and much skill: to make another thing requires very little labor and no skill out of the common. Here then is your basis of value, obvious and beyond argument. A primitive savage makes a bow and arrow in a day: it takes him a fortnight to make a bark canoe. On that fact rests the exchange value between the two. The relative quantity of labor embodied in each object is the basis of its value.

This line of reasoning has a very convincing

sound.    It appears in nearly every book on economic theory from Adam Smith and Ricardo
till to-day. "Labor alone," wrote Smith,
"never varying in its own value is above the
ultimate and real standard by which the value
of all commodities can at all times and places
be estimated and compared."

But the idea that *quantity of labor governs*
value will not stand examination for a moment.
What is *quantity* of labor and how is it measured?    As long as we draw our illustrations
from primitive life where one man's work is
much the same as another's and where all oper-
ations are simple, we seem easily able to measure and compare.    One day is the same as another and one man about as capable as his fellow.    But in the complexity of modern industrial life such a calculation no longer applies:
the differences of skill, of native ingenuity, and
technical preparation become enormous.    The
hour's work of a common laborer is not the
same thing as the hour's work of a watchmaker
mending a watch, or of an engineer directing
the building of a bridge, or of an architect

drawing a plan. There is no way of reducing these hours to a common basis. We may think, if we like, that the quantity of labor *ought* to be the basis of value and exchange. Such is always the dream of the socialist. But on a closer view it is shattered like any other dream. For we have, alas, no means of finding out what the quantity of labor is and how it can be measured. We cannot measure it in terms of time. We have no calculus for comparing relative amounts of skill and energy. We can not measure it by the amount of its contribution to the product, for that is the very matter that we want to discover.

What the economist does is to slip out of the difficulty altogether by begging the whole question. He deliberately measures the quantity of labor *by what is paid for it.* Skilled labor is worth, let us say, three times as much as common labor; and brain work, speaking broadly, is worth several times as much again. Hence by adding up all the wages and salaries paid we get something that seems to indicate the total quantity of labor, measured not simply in time, but with an allowance for skill and technical competency. By describing this allowance as a coefficient we can give our statement a false air of mathematical certainty and so muddle up the essential question that the truth is lost from sight like a pea under a thimble. Now you see it and now you don't. The thing is, in fact, a mere piece of intellectual conjuring. The conjurer has slipped the phrase, "quantity of labor," up his sleeve, and when it reappears it has turned into "the expense of hiring labor." This is a quite different thing. But as both conceptions are related somehow to the idea of cost, the substitution is never discovered.

On this false basis a vast structure is erected. All prices, provided that competition is free, are made to appear as the necessary result of natural forces. They are "natural" or "normal" prices. All wages are explained, and low wages are exonerated, on what seems to be an undeniable ground of fact. They are what they are. You may wish them otherwise, but they are not. As a philanthropist, you may feel sorry that a humble laborer should work through a long day to receive two dollars, but as an economist you console yourself with the reflection that that is all he produces. You may at times, as a sentimentalist, wonder whether the vast sums drawn as interest on capital are consistent with social fairness; but if it is shown that interest is simply the "natural price" of capital representing the actual "productive power" of the capital, there is nothing further to say. You may have similar qualms over rent and the rightness and wrongness of it. The enormous "unearned increment" that accrues for the fortunate owner of land who toils not neither spins to obtain it, may seem difficult of justification. But after all, land is only one particular case of ownership under the one and the same system. The rent for which the owner can lease it, emerges simply as a consequence of the existing state of wages and prices. High rent, says the economist, does not make big prices: it merely follows as a consequence or result of them. Dear bread is not caused by the high rents paid by

tenant farmers for the land: the train of cause
and effect runs in the contrary direction. And
the selling price of land is merely a consequence
of its rental value, a simple case of capitaliza-
tion of annual return into a present sum.   City
land, though it looks different from farm land,
is seen in the light of this same analysis, to earn
its rent in just the same way.   The high rent
of a Broadway store, says the economist, does
not add a single cent to the price of the things
sold in it.   It is because prices are what they
are that the rent is and can be paid.   Hence
on examination the same canon of social justice
that covers and explains prices, wages, and interest applies with perfect propriety to rent.

Or finally, to take the strongest case of all,
one may, as a citizen, feel apprehension at times
at the colossal fortune of a Carnegie or a Rockefeller.   For it does seem passing strange that
one human being should control as property the
mass of coin, goods, houses, factories, land and
mines, represented by a billion dollars; stranger
still that at his death he should write upon a
piece of paper his commands as to what his sur-

viving fellow creatures are to do with it. But
if it can be shown to be true that Mr. Rockefeller "made" his fortune in the same sense that
a man makes a log house by felling trees and
putting them one upon another, then the fortune belongs to Mr. Rockefeller in the same
way as the log house belongs to the pioneer.
And if the social inferences that are drawn
from the theory of natural liberty and natural
value are correct, the millionaire and the landlord, the plutocrat and the pioneer, the wage
earner and the capitalist, have each all the right
to do what he will with his own. For every
man in this just world gets what is coming to
him. He gets what he is worth, and he is
worth what he gets.

But if one knocks out the keystone of the
arch in the form of a proposition that natural
value conforms to the cost of production, then
the whole edifice collapses and must be set up
again, upon another plan and on another foun-
dation, stone by stone.

## IV.—Work and Wages

WAGES and prices, then, if the argument recited in the preceding chapter of this series holds good, do not under free competition tend towards social justice. It is not true that every man gets what he produces. It is not true that enormous salaries represent enormous productive services and that humble wages correspond to a humble contribution to the welfare of society. Prices, wages, salaries, interest, rent and profits do not, if left to themselves, follow the simple law of natural justice. To think so is an idle dream, the dream of the quietist who may slumber too long and be roused to a rude awakening or perish, perhaps, in his sleep. His dream is not so dangerous as the contrasted dream of the socialist, now threatening to walk abroad in his sleep, but both in their degree are dreams and nothing more.

The real truth is that prices and wages are all the various payments from hand to hand in industrial society, are the outcome of a complex of competing forces that are not based upon justice but upon "economic strength." To elucidate this it is necessary to plunge into the jungle of pure economic theory. The way is arduous. There are no flowers upon the path. And out of this thicket, alas, no two people ever emerge hand in hand in concord. Yet it is a path that must be traversed. Let us take, then, as a beginning the very simplest case of the making of a price. It is the one which is sometimes called in books on economics the case of an unique monopoly. Suppose that I offer for sale the manuscript of the Pickwick Papers, or Shakespere's skull, or, for the matter of that, the skull of John Smith, what is the sum that I shall receive for it? It is the utmost that any one is willing to give for it. That is all one can say about it. There is no question here of cost or what I paid for the article or of anything else except the amount of the willingness to pay on the part of the highest bidder. It would be possible, indeed, for a bidder to take the article from me by force. But this we presume to be prevented by the law, and for this reason we referred above not to the physical strength, but to the "economic strength" of the parties to a bargain. By this is meant the relation that arises out of the condition of the supply and the demand, the willingness or eagerness, or the sheer necessity, of the buyers and the sellers. People may offer much because the thing to be acquired is an absolute necessity without which they perish; a drowning man would sell all that he had for a life belt. Or they may offer much through the sheer abundance of their other possessions. A millionaire might offer more for a life belt as a souvenir than a drowning man could pay for it to save his life.

Yet out of any particular conjunction between desires on the one hand and goods or services on the other arises a particular equation of demand and supply, represented by a particular price. All of this, of course, is A. B. C., and I am not aware that anybody doubts it.

Now let us make the example a little more elaborate. Suppose that one single person owned all the food supply of a community isolated from the outside world. The price which he could exact would be the full measure of all the possessions of his neighbors up to the point at least where they would commit suicide rather than pay. True, in such a case as this, "economic strength" would probably be broken down by the intrusion of physical violence. But in so far as it held good the price of food would be based upon it.

Prices such as are indicated here were dismissed by the earlier economist as mere economic curiosities. John Stuart Mill has something to say about the price of a "music box in the wilds of Lake Superior," which, as he perceived, would not be connected with the expense of producing it, but might be vastly more or perhaps decidedly less. But Mill might have said the same thing about the price of a music box, provided it was properly patented, anywhere at all. For the music box and Shakespere's skull and the corner in wheat are all merely different kinds of examples of the things called a monopoly sale.

Now let us change the example a little further. Suppose that the monopolist has for sale not simply a fixed and definite quantity of a certain article, but something which he can produce in larger quantities as desired. At what price will he now sell? If he offers the article at a very high price only a few people will take it: if he lowers the price there will be more and more purchasers. His interest seems divided. He will want to put the price as high as possible so that the profit on each single article (over what it costs him to produce it) will be as great as possible. But he will also want to make as many sales as he possibly can, which will induce him to set the price low enough to bring in new buyers. But, of course, if he puts the price so low that it only covers the cost of making the goods his profit is all gone and the mere multiplicity of sales is no good to him. He must try therefore to find a point of maximum profit where, having in view both the number of sales and the profit over cost on each sale the net profit is at its greatest. This gives us the fundamental law of monopoly price. It is to be noted that under modern conditions of production the cost of manufacture per article decreases to a great extent in proportion as a larger and larger number is produced and thus the widening of the sale lowers the proportionate cost. In any particular case, therefore, it may turn out that the price that suits the monopolist's own interest is quite a low price, one such as to allow for an enormous quantity of sales and a very low cost of manufacture. This, we say, *may* be the case. But it is not so of necessity. In and of itself the monopoly price corresponds to the monopolist's profit and not to cheapness of sale. The price *may* be set far above the cost.

And now notice the peculiar relation that is set up between the monopolist's production and the satisfaction of human wants. In proportion as the quantity produced is increased the lower must the price be set in order to sell the whole output. If the monopolist insisted on turning out more and more of his goods, the price that people would give would fall until it barely covered the cost, then till it was less than cost, then to a mere fraction of the cost and finally to nothing at all. In other words, if one produces a large enough quantity of anything it becomes worthless. It loses all its value just as soon as there is enough of it to satisfy, and over-satisfy the wants of humanity. Thus if the world produces three and a half billion bushels of wheat it can be sold, let us say, at two dollars a bushel; but if it produced twice as much it might well be found that it would only sell for fifty cents a bushel. The value of the bigger supply as a total would actually be less than that of the smaller. And if the supply were big enough it would be worth, in the economic sense, just nothing at all. This peculiarity is spoken of in economic theory as the paradox of value. It is referred to in the older books either as an economic curiosity or as a mere illustration in extreme terms of the relation of supply to price. Thus in many books the story is related of how the East India Companies used at times deliberately to destroy a large quantity of tea in order that by selling a lesser amount they might reap a larger profit than by selling a greater.

But in reality this paradox of value is the most fundamental proposition in economic science. Precisely here is found the key to the operation of the economic society in which we live. The world's production is aimed at producing "values," not in producing plenty. If by some mad access of misdirected industry we produced enough and too much of everything, our whole machinery of buying and selling would break down. This indeed does happen constantly on a small scale in the familiar phenomenon of over-production. But in the organization in which we live over-production tends to check itself at once. If the world's machinery threatens to produce a too great plenty of any particular thing, then it turns itself towards producing something else of which there is not yet enough. This is done quite unconsciously without any philanthropic intent on the part of the individual producer and without any general direction in the way of a social command. The machine does it of itself. When there is *enough* the wheels slacken and stop. This sounds at first hearing most admirable. But let it be noted that the *"enough"* here in question does not mean enough to satisfy human wants. In fact it means precisely the converse. It means enough *not* to satisfy them, and to leave the selling price of the things made at the point of profit.

Let it be observed also that we have hitherto been speaking as if all things were produced under a monopoly. The objection might at once be raised that with competitive producers the price will also keep falling down towards cost and will not be based upon the point of maximum profit. We shall turn to this objection in a moment. But one or two other points must be considered before doing so.

In the first place in following out such an argument as the present in regard to the peculiar shortcomings of the system under which we live, it is necessary again and again to warn the reader against a hasty conclusion to the possibilities of altering and amending it. The socialist reads such criticism as the above with impatient approval. "Very well," he says, "the whole organization is wrong and works badly. Now let us abolish it altogether and make a better one." But in doing so he begs the whole question at issue. The point is, *can* we make a better one or must we be content with patching up the old one? Take an illustration. Scientists tell us that from the point of view of optics the human eye is a clumsy instrument poorly contrived for its work. A certain great authority once said that if he had made it he would have been ashamed of it. This may be true. But the eye unfortunately is all we have to see by. If we destroy our eyes in the hope of making better ones we may go blind. The best that we can do is to improve our sight by adding a pair of spectacles. So it is with the organization of society. Faulty though it is, it does the work after a certain fashion. We may apply to it with advantage the spectacles of social reform, but what the socialist offers us is total blindness. But of this presently.

To return to the argument. Let us consider next what wages the monopolist in the cases described above will have to pay. We take for granted that he will only pay as much as he has to. How much will this be? Clearly enough it will depend altogether on the number of available working men capable of doing the work in question and the situation in which they find themselves. It is again a case of relative "economic strength." The situation may be altogether in favor of the employer or altogether in favor of the men, or may occupy a middle ground. If the men are so numerous that there are more of them than are needed for the work, and if there is no other occupation for them they must accept a starvation wage. If they are so few in number that they can *all* be employed, and if they are so well organized as to act together, they can in their turn exact any wage up to the point that leaves no profit for the employer himself at all. Indeed for a short time wages might even pass this point, the monopolist employer being willing (for various reasons, all quite obvious) actually to pay more as wages than he gets as return and to carry on business at a loss for the sake of carrying it on at all. Clearly, then, wages, as Adam Smith said, "are the result of a dispute" in which either party must be pushed to the wall. The employer may have to pay so much that there is nothing or practically nothing left for himself, or so little that his workmen can just exist and no more. These are the upward and downward limits of the wages in the cases described.

It is therefore obvious that if all the industries in the world were carried on as a series of separate monopolies, there would be exactly the kind of rivalry or competition of forces represented by the consumer insisting on paying as little as possible, the producer charging the most profitable price and paying the lowest wage that he could, and the wage earner demanding the highest wage that he could get.

The equilibrium would be an unstable one.  It would be constantly displaced and shifted by the movement of all sorts of social forces—by changes of fashion, by abundance or scarcity of crops, by alterations in the technique of industry and by the cohesion or the slackening of the organization of any group of workers.  But the balanced forces once displaced would be seen constantly to come to an equilibrium at a new point.

All this has been said of industry under monopoly.  But it will be seen to apply in its essentials to what we call competitive industry. Here indeed certain new features come in. Not one employer but many produce each kind of article.  And, as far as each employer can see by looking at his own horizon, what he does is merely to produce as much as he can sell at a price that pays him.  Since all the other employers are doing this, there will be, under competition, a constant tendency to cut the prices down to the lowest that is consistent with what the employer has to pay as wages and interest.  This point, which was called by the orthodox economists the "cost," is not in any true and fundamental sense of the words the "cost" at all. It is merely a limit represented by what the other parties to the bargain are able to exact. The whole situation is in a condition of unstable equilibrium in which the conflicting forces represented by the interests of the various parties pull in different directions. The employers in any one line of industry and all their wage earners and salaried assistants have one and the same interest as against the consumer. They want the selling price to be as high as possible. But the employers are against one another as wanting, each of them, to make as many sales as possible, and each and all the employers are against the wage earners in wanting to pay as low wages as possible. If all the employers unite, the situation turns to a monopoly, and the price paid by the consumer is settled on the monopoly basis already described. The employers can then dispute it out with their working men as to how much wages shall be. If the employers are not united, then at each and every moment they are in conflict both with the consumer and with their wage earners. Thus the whole scene of industry represents a vast and unending conflict, a fermentation in which the moving bubbles crowd for space, expanding and breaking one against the other. There is no point of rest. There is no real fixed "cost" acting as a basis. Anything that any one person or group of persons—worker or master, landlord or capitalist—is able to exact owing to the existing conditions of demand or supply, becomes a "cost" from the point of view of all the others. There is nothing in this "cost" which proportions to it the quantity of labor, or of time, or of skill or of any other measure physical or psychological of the effort involved. And there is nothing whatever in it which proportions to it social justice. It is the war of each against all. Its only mitigation is that it is carried on under the set of rules represented by the state and the law.

The tendencies involved may be best illustrated by taking one or two extreme or exaggerated examples, not meant as facts but only to make clear the nature of social and industrial forces among which we live.

What, for example, will be the absolute maximum to which wages in general could be forced? Conceivably and in the purest and thinnest of theory, they could include the whole product of the labor of society with just such a small fraction left over for the employers, the owners of capital and the owners of land to induce them to continue acting as part of the machine. That is to say, if all the laborers all over the world, to the last one, were united under a single control they could force the other economic classes of society to something approaching a starvation living. In practice this is nonsense. In theory it is an excellent starting point for thought.

And how short could the hours of the universal united workers be made? As short as ever they liked: An hour a day: ten minutes, anything they like; but of course with the proviso that the shorter the hours the less the total of things produced to be divided. It is true that up to a certain point shortening the hours of labor actually increases the total product. A ten-hour day, speaking in general terms and leaving out individual exceptions, is probably more productive than a day of twelve. It may very well be that an eight-hour day will prove, presently if not immediately, to be more productive than one of ten. But somewhere the limit is reached and gross production falls. The supply of things in general gets shorter. But note that this itself would not matter much, if somehow and in some way not yet found, the shortening of the production of goods cut out the luxuries and superfluities first. Mankind at large might well trade leisure for luxuries. The shortening of hours with the correspond- ·ing changes in the direction of production is really the central problem in social reform. I propose to return to it in the concluding chapter of these papers, but for the present it is only noted in connection with the general scheme of industrial relations.

Now let us ask to what extent any particular section or part of industrial society can suc- ceed in forcing up wages or prices as against the others. In pure theory they may do this almost to any extent, provided that the thing concerned is a necessity and is without a substitute and provided that their organization is complete and unbreakable. If all the people concerned in producing coal, masters and men, owners of mines and operators of machinery, could stand out for their price, there is no limit, short of putting all the rest of the world on starvation rations, to what they might get. In practice and in reality a thousand things intervene—the impossibility of such complete unity, the organization of the other parties, the existing of national divisions among industrial society, sentiment, decency, fear. The proposition is only "pure theory." But its use as such is to dispose of any such idea as that there is a natural price of coal or of anything else.

The above is true of any article of necessity. It is true though in a less degree of things of luxury. If all the makers of instruments of music, masters and men, capitalists and workers, were banded together in a tight and unbreakable union, then the other economic

classes must either face the horrors of a world
without pianolas and trombones, or hand over
the price demanded. And what is true of coal
and music is true all through the whole mechanism of industry.

Or take the supreme case of the owners of
land. If all of them acted together, with their
legal rights added into one, they could order
the rest of the world either to get off it or to
work at starvation wages.

Industrial society is therefore mobile, elastic,
standing at any moment in a temporary and
unstable equilibrium. But at any particular
moment the possibility of a huge and catastro-
phic shift such as those described is out of the
question except at the price of a general col-
lapse. Even a minor dislocation breaks down
a certain part of the machinery of society.
Particular groups of workers are thrown out
of place. There is no other place where they
can fit in, or at any rate not immediately. The
machine labors heavily. Ominous mutterings
are heard. The legal framework of the State
and of obedience to the law in which indus-

trial society is set threatens to break asunder.
The attempt at social change threatens a social
revolution in which the whole elaborate mechanism would burst into fragments.

In any social movement, then, change and
alteration in a new direction must be balanced
against the demands of social stability. Some
things are possible and some are not; some are
impossible to-day, and possible or easy to-
morrow. Others are forever out of the question.

But this much at least ought to appear clear
if the line of argument indicated above is accepted, namely, that there is no great hope for
universal betterment of society by the mere advance of technical industrial progress and by
the unaided play of the motive of every man
for himself.

The enormous increase in the productivity
of industrial effort would never of itself have
elevated by one inch the lot of the working
class. The rise of wages in the nineteenth century and the shortening of hours that went
with it was due neither to the advance in me-

chanical power nor to the advance in diligence
and industriousness, nor to the advance, if
there was any, in general kindliness. It was
due to the organization of labor. Mechanical
progress makes higher wages possible. It does
not, of itself, advance them by a single farthing.
Labor saving machinery does not of itself save
the working world a single hour of toil: it only
shifts it from one task to another.

Against a system of unrestrained individualism, energy, industriousness and honesty might
shatter itself in vain. The thing is merely a
race in which only one can be first no matter
how great the speed of all; a struggle in which
one, and not all, can stand upon the shoulders
of the others. It is the restriction of individualism by the force of organization and by legislation that has brought to the world whatever social advance has been achieved by the
great mass of the people.

The present moment is in a sense the wrong
time to say this. We no longer live in an age
when down-trodden laborers meet by candle-
light with the ban of the law upon their meet-

ing. These are the days when "labor" is triumphant, and when it ever threatens in the overweening strength of its own power to break industrial society in pieces in the fierce attempt to do in a day what can only be done in a generation. But truth is truth. And any one who writes of the history of the progress of industrial society owes it to the truth to acknowledge the vast social achievement of organized labor in the past.

And what of the future?

By what means and in what stages can social progress be further accelerated? This I propose to treat in the succeeding chapters, dealing first with the proposals of the socialists and the revolutionaries, and finally with the prospect for a sane, orderly and continuous social reform.

## V.—The Land of Dreams: The Utopia of the Socialist

WHO is there that has not turned at times from the fever and fret of the world we live in, from the spectacle of its wasted energy, its wild frenzy of work and its bitter inequality, to the land of dreams, to the pictured vision of the world as it might be?

Such a vision has haunted in all ages the brooding mind of mankind; and every age has fashioned for itself the image of a "somewhere" or "nowhere"—a Utcpia in which there should be equality and justice for all. The vision itself is an outcome of that divine discontent which raises man above his environment.

Every age has had its socialism, its communism, its dream of bread and work for all.

But the dream has varied always in the likeness of the thought of the time. In earlier days the dream was not one of social wealth. It was rather a vision of the abnegation of riches, of humble possessions shared in common after the manner of the unrealized ideal of the Christian faith. It remained for the age of machinery and power to bring forth another and a vastly more potent socialism. This was no longer a plan whereby all might be poor together, but a proposal that all should be rich together. The collectivist state advocated by the socialist of to-day has scarcely anything in common with the communism of the middle ages.

Modern socialism is the direct outcome of the age of machine production. It takes its first inspiration from glaring contrasts between riches and poverty presented by the modern era, from the strange paradox that has been described above between human power and its failure to satisfy human want. The nineteenth century brought with it the factory and the factory slavery of the Lancashire children, the

modern city and city slum, the plutocracy and
the proletariat, and all the strange discrepancy
between wealth and want that has disfigured
the material progress of the last hundred years.
The rising splendor of capitalism concealed
from the dazzled eye the melancholy spectacle
of the new industrial poverty that lay in the
shadow behind it.

The years that followed the close of the
Napoleonic wars in 1815 were in many senses
years of unexampled misery. The accumulated burden of the war lay heavy upon Europe.
The rise of the new machine power had dis-
located the older system. A multitude of land-
less men clamored for bread and work. Pauperism spread like a plague. Each new invention threw thousands of hand-workers out of
employment. The law still branded as conspiracy any united attempt of workingmen to
raise wages or to shorten the hours of work.
At the very moment when the coming of steam
power and the use of modern machinery were
piling up industrial fortunes undreamed of before, destitution, pauperism and unemployment

seemed more widespread and more ominous than ever. In this rank atmosphere germinated modern socialism. The writings of Marx and Engels and Louis Blanc were inspired by what they saw about them.

From its very cradle socialism showed the double aspect which has distinguished it ever since. To the minds of some it was the faith of the insurrectionist, something to be achieved by force; "bourgeois" society must be overthrown by force of arms; if open and fair fighting was not possible against such great odds, it must be blown skyhigh with gunpowder. Dynamite, by the good fortune of invention, came to the revolutionary at the very moment when it was most wanted. To the men of violence, socialism was the twin brother of anarchism, born at the same time, advocating the same means and differing only as to the final end.

But to others, socialism was from the beginning, as it is to-day, a creed of peace. It advocated the betterment of society not by violence but by persuasion, by peaceful argument and

the recognized rule of the majority.    It is true
that the earlier socialists almost to a man in-
cluded, in the first passion of their denunciation,
things not necessarily within the compass of
purely economic reform.    As children of misery they cried out against all human institutions.    The bond of marriage seemed an ac-
cursed thing, the mere slavery of women.    The
family—the one institution in which the better
side of human nature shines with an undimmed
light—was to them but an engine of class op-
pression; the Christian churches merely the par-
asitic servants of the tyrannous power of a
plutocratic state.    The whole history of human
civilization was denounced as an unredeemed
record of the spoliation of the weak by the
strong.    Even the domain of the philosopher
was needlessly invaded and all forms of spec-
ulative belief were rudely thrown aside in favor
of a wooden materialism as dogmatic as any
of the creeds or theories which it proposed to
replace.

Thus seen, socialism appeared as the very
antithesis of law and order, of love and chas-

tity, and of religion itself. It was a tainted creed. There was blood upon its hands and bloody menace in its thoughts. It was a thing to be stamped out, to be torn up by the roots. The very soil in which it grew must be burned out with the flame of avenging justice.

Such it still appears to many people to-day. The unspeakable savagery of bolshevism has made good the wildest threats of the partisans of violence and fulfilled the sternest warnings of the conservative. To-day more than ever socialism is in danger of becoming a prescribed creed, its very name under the ban of the law, its literature burned by the hangman and a gag placed upon its mouth.

But this is neither right nor wise. Socialism, like every other impassioned human effort, will flourish best under martyrdom. It will languish and perish in the dry sunlight of open discussion.

For it must always be remembered in fairness that the creed of violence has no necessary connection with socialism. In its essential nature socialism is nothing but a proposal for cer-

tain kinds of economic reform.    A man has
just as much right to declare himself a socialist
as he has to call himself a Seventh Day Advent-
ist or a Prohibitionist, or a Perpetual Motion-
ist.    It is, or should be, open to him to convert
others to his way of thinking.    It is only time
to restrain him when he proposes to convert
others by means of a shotgun or by dynamite,
and by forcible interference with their own
rights.    When he does this he ceases to be a
socialist pure and simple and becomes a criminal as well.    The law can deal with him as
such.

But with socialism itself the law, in a free
country, should have no kind of quarrel.    For
in the whole program of peaceful socialism
there is nothing wrong at all except one thing.
Apart from this it is a high and ennobling ideal
truly fitted for a community of saints.    And
the one thing that is wrong with socialism is
that it won't work.    That is all.    It is, as it
were, a beautiful machine of which the wheels,
dependent upon some unknown and uninvented
motive power, refuse to turn.    The unknown

motive force in this case means a power of altruism, of unselfishness, of willingness to labor for the good of others, such as the human race has never known, nor is ever likely to know. But the worst public policy to pursue in reference to such a machine is to lock it up, to prohibit all examination of it and to allow it to become a hidden mystery, the whispered hope of its martyred advocates. Better far to stand it out into the open daylight, to let all who will inspect it, and to prove even to the simplest that such a contrivance once and for all and for ever cannot be made to run.

Let us turn to examine the machine.

We may omit here all discussion of the historical progress of socialism and the stages whereby it changed from the creed of a few theorists and revolutionists to being the accepted platform of great political parties, counting its adherents by the million. All of this belongs elsewhere. It suffices here to note that in the process of its rise it has chafed away much of the superfluous growth that clung to it and has become a purely economic doctrine.

There is no longer any need to discuss in connection with it the justification of marriage and the family, and the rightness or wrongness of Christianity: no need to decide whether the materialistic theory of history is true or false, since nine socialists out of ten to-day have forgotten, or have never heard, what the materialistic theory of history is: no need to examine whether human history is, or is not, a mere record of class exploitation, since the controversy has long shifted to other grounds. The essential thing to-day is not the past, but the future. The question is, what does the socialist have to say about the conditions under which we live and the means that he advocates for the betterment of them?

His case stands thus. He begins his discussion with an indictment of the manifold weaknesses and the obvious injustices of the system under which we live. And in this the socialist is very largely right. He shows that under free individual competition there is a perpetual waste of energy. Competing rivals cover the same field. Even the simplest services are performed with an almost ludicrous waste of energy. In every modern city the milk supply is distributed by erratic milkmen who skip from door to door and from street to street, covering the same ground, each leaving his cans of milk here and there in a sporadic fashion as haphazard as a bee among the flowers. Contrast, says the socialist, the wasted labors of the milkman with the orderly and systematic performance of the postman, himself a little fragment of socialism. And the milkman, they tell us, is typical of modern industrial society. Competing railways run trains on parallel tracks, with empty cars that might be filled and with vast executive organizations which do ten times over the work that might be done by one. Competing stores needlessly occupy the time of hundreds of thousands of employees in a mixture of idleness and industry. An inconceivable quantity of human effort is spent on advertising, mere shouting and display, as unproductive in the social sense as the beating of a drum. Competition breaks into a dozen inefficient parts the process that might conceivably be carried out, with an infinite saving of effort, by a single guiding hand.

The socialist looking thus at the world we live in sees in it nothing but waste and selfishness and inefficiency. He looks so long that a mist comes before his eyes. He loses sight of the supreme fact that after all, in its own poor, clumsy fashion, the machine does work. He loses sight of the possibility of our falling into social chaos. He sees no longer the brink of the abyss beside which the path of progress picks its painful way. He leaps with a shout of exultation over the cliff.

And he lands, at least in imagination, in his ideal state, his Utopia. Here the noise and clamor of competitive industry is stilled. We look about us at a peaceful landscape where men and women brightly clothed and abundantly fed and warmed, sing at their easy task. There is enough for all and more than enough. Poverty has vanished. Want is unknown. The children play among the flowers. The youths and maidens are at school. There are no figures here bent with premature toil, no

## VI.—How Mr. Bellamy Looked Backward

THE reading public is as wayward and as fickle as a bee among the flowers. It will not long pause anywhere, and it easily leaves each blossom for a better. But like the bee, while impelled by an instinct that makes it search for sugar, it sucks in therewith its solid sustenance.

I am not quite certain that the bee does exactly do this; but it is just the kind of thing that the bee is likely to do. And in any case it is precisely the thing which the reading public does. It will not read unless it is tempted by the sugary sweetness of the romantic interest. It must have its hero and its heroine and its course of love that never will run smooth. For information the reader cares nothing. If he absorbs it, it must be by accident, and unawares. He passes over the heavy tomes filled

with valuable fact, and settles like the random
bee upon the bright flowers of contemporary
romance.

Hence if the reader is to be ensnared into
absorbing something useful, it must be hidden
somehow among the flowers. A treatise on
religion must be disguised as a love story in
which a young clergyman, sworn into holy
orders, falls in love with an actress. The
facts of history are imparted by a love story
centering around the adventures of a hitherto
unknown son of Louis the Fourteenth. And
a discussion of the relations of labor and capital takes the form of a romance in which the
daughter of a multi-millionaire steps volunta-
rily out of her Fifth Avenue home to work in
a steam laundry.

Such is the recognized method by which the
great unthinking public is taught to think.
Slavery was not fully known till Mrs. Stowe
wrote "Uncle Tom's Cabin," and the slow
tyranny of the law's delay was taught to the
world for ever in the pages of "Bleak House."

So it has been with socialism. No single

influence ever brought its ideas and its propaganda so forcibly and clearly before the public mind as Mr. Edward Bellamy's brilliant novel, "Looking Backward," published some thirty years ago. The task was arduous. Social and economic theory is heavy to the verge of being indigestible. There is no such thing as a gay book on political economy for reading in a hammock. Yet Mr. Bellamy succeeded. His book is in cold reality nothing but a series of conversations explaining how a socialist commonwealth is supposed to work. Yet he contrives to bring into it a hero and a heroine, and somehow the warm beating of their hearts and the stolen glances in their eyes breathe into the dry dust of economic argument the breath of life. Nor was ever a better presentation made of the essential program of socialism.

It is worth while then, as was said in the preceding chapter, to consider Mr. Bellamy's commonwealth as the most typical and the most carefully constructed of all the ready-made socialisms that have been put forward.

The mere machinery of the story can be

lightly passed over. It is intended simply as
the sugar that lures the random bee. The
hero, living in Boston in 1887, is supposed to
fall asleep in a deep, underground chamber
which he has made for himself as a remedy
against a harassing insomnia. Unknown to
the sleeper the house above his retreat is
burned down. He remains in a trance for a
hundred and thirteen years and awakes to find
himself in the Boston of the year 2000 A. D.
Kind hands remove him from his sepulcher.
He is revived. He finds himself under the
care of a certain learned and genial Dr. Leete,
whose house stands on the very site where once
the sleeper lived. The beautiful daughter of
Dr. Leete looks upon the newcomer from the
lost world with eyes in which, to the mind of
the sagacious reader, love is seen at once to
dawn. In reality she is the great-granddaughter
of the fiancée whom the sleeper was to have
married in his former life; thus a faint sugges-
tion of the transmigration of souls illuminates
their intercourse. Beyond that there is no
story and at the end of the book the sleeper,

in another dream, is conveniently transported back to 1887 which he can now contrast, in horror, with the ideal world of 2000 A. D.

And what was this world? The sleeper's first vision of it was given him by Dr. Leete, who took him to the house top and let him see the Boston of the future. Wide avenues replace the crowded, noisy streets. There are no shops but only here and there among the trees great marble buildings, the emporiums from which the goods are delivered to the purple public.

And the goods are delivered indeed! Dr. Leete explains it all with intervals of grateful cigar smoking and of music and promenades with the beautiful Edith, and meals in wonderful communistic restaurants with romantic waiters, who feel themselves, *mirabile dictu,* quite independent.

And this is how the commonwealth operates. Everybody works or at least works until the age of forty, so that it may be truly said in these halcyon days everybody works but father. But the work of life does not begin till education

ends at the age of twenty-one.  After that all
the young men and women pass for three years
into the general "Industrial Army," much as
the young men used to pass into the ranks of
conscription.  Afterwards each person may se-
lect any trade that he likes.  But the hours are
made longer or shorter according to whether
too many or too few young people apply to
come in.  A gardener works for more hours
than a scavenger.  Yet all occupations are
equally honorable.  The wages of all the people are equal; or rather there are no wages at
all, as the workers merely receive cards, which
entitle them to goods of such and such a quantity at any of the emporiums.  The cards are
punched out as the goods are used.  The goods
are all valued according to the amount of time
used in their making and each citizen draws
out the same total amount.  But he may take
it out in installments just as he likes, drawing
many things one month and few the next.  He
may even get goods in advance if he has any
special need.  He may, within a certain time
limit, save up his cards, but it must be remem-

bered that the one thing which no card can buy
and which no citizens can own is the "means
of production." These belong collectively to
all. Land, mines, machinery, factories and the
whole mechanism of transport, these things are
public property managed by the State. Its
workers in their use of them are all directed
by public authority as to what they shall make
and when they shall make it, and how much
shall be made. On these terms all share alike;
the cripple receives as much as the giant; the
worker of exceptional dexterity and energy the
same as his slower and less gifted fellow.

All the management, the control—and let
this be noted, for there is no escape from it
either by Mr. Bellamy or by anybody else—
is exercised by boards of officials elected by the
people. All the complex organization by
which production goes on by which the workers
are supervised and shifted from trade to trade,
by which their requests for a change of work
or an extension of credit are heard and judged
—all of this is done by the elected "bosses."
One lays stress on this not because it is Mr.

Bellamy's plan, but because it is, and it *has to be,* the plan of anybody who constructs a social-ist commonwealth.

Mr. Bellamy has many ingenious arrange-ments to meet the needs of people who want to be singers or actors or writers,—in other words, who do not want to work. They may sing or act as much as they like, provided that enough other people will hand over enough of their food cards to keep them going. But if no one wants to hear them sing or see them act they may starve,—just as they do now. Here the author harks back unconsciously to his nine-teenth century individualism; he need not have done so; other socialist writers would have it that one of the everlasting boards would "sit on" every aspiring actor or author before he was allowed to begin. But we may take it either way. It is not the major point. There is no need to discuss the question of how to deal with the artist under socialism. If the rest of it were all right, no one need worry about the artist. Perhaps he would do better without being remunerated at all. It is doubtful whether the huge commercial premium that greets success to-day does good or harm. But let it pass. It is immaterial to the present matter.

One comes back to the essential question of the structure of the commonwealth. Can such a thing, or anything conceived in its likeness, possibly work? The answer is, and must be, absolutely and emphatically no.

Let anyone conversant with modern democracy as it is,—not as its founders dreamed of it,—picture to himself the operation of a system whereby anything and everything is controlled by elected officials, from whom there is no escape, outside of whom is no livelihood and to whom all men must bow! Democracy, let us grant it, is the best system of government as yet operative in this world of sin. Beside autocratic kingship it shines with a white light; it is obviously the portal of the future. But we know it now too well to idealize its merits.

A century and a half ago when the world was painfully struggling out of the tyranny of autocratic kingship, when English liberalism was in its cradle, when Thomas Jefferson was composing the immortal phrases of the Declaration of Independence and unknown patriots dreamed of freedom in France,—at such an epoch it was but natural that the principle of popular election should be idealized as the sovereign remedy for the political evils of mankind. It was natural and salutary that it should be so. The force of such idealization helped to carry forward the human race to a new milestone on the path of progress.

But when it is proposed to entrust to the method of elective control not a part but the whole of the fortunes of humanity, to commit to it not merely the form of government and the necessary maintenance of law, order and public safety, but the whole operation of the production and distribution of the world's goods, the case is altered. The time is ripe then for retrospect over the experience of the nineteenth century and for a realization of what has proved in that experience the peculiar defects of elective democracy.

Mr. Bellamy pictures his elected managers,

—as every socialist has to do,—as a sagacious
and paternal group, free from the interest of
self and the play of the baser passions and animated only by the thought of the public good.
Gravely they deliberate; wisely and justly they
decide. Their gray heads—for Bellamy prefers them old—are bowed in quiet confabula-
tion over the nice adjustment of the national
production, over the petition of this or that
citizen. The public care sits heavily on their
breast. Their own peculiar fortune they have
lightly passed by. They do not favor their
relations or their friends. They do not count
their hours of toil. They do not enumerate
their gain. They work, in short, as work the
angels.

Now let me ask in the name of sanity where
are such officials to be found? Here and
there, perhaps, one sees in the world of to-day
in the stern virtue of an honorable public ser-
vant some approximation to such a civic ideal.
But how much, too, has been seen of the rule
of "cliques" and "interests" and "bosses;" of
the election of genial incompetents popular as

spendthrifts; of crooked partisans warm to their friends and bitter to their enemies; of administration by a party for a party; and of the insidious poison of commercial greed defiling the wells of public honesty. The unending conflict between business and politics, between the private gain and the public good, has been for two generations the despair of modern democracy. It turns this way and that in its vain effort to escape corruption. It puts its faith now in representative legislatures, and now in appointed boards and commissions; it appeals to the vote of the whole people or it places an almost autocratic power and a supreme responsibility in the hands of a single man. And nowhere has the escape been found. The melancholy lesson is being learned that the path of human progress is arduous and its forward movement slow and that no mere form of government can aid unless it is inspired by a higher public spirit of the individual citizen than we have yet managed to achieve.

And of the world of to-day, be it remembered, elective democratic control covers only a part of the field. Under socialism it covers it all. To-day in our haphazard world a man is his own master; often indeed the mastership is but a pitiful thing, little more than being master of his own failure and starvation; often indeed the dead weight of circumstance, the accident of birth, the want of education, may so press him down that his freedom is only a mockery. Let us grant all that. But under socialism freedom is gone. There is nothing but the rule of the elected boss. The worker is commanded to his task and obey he must. If he will not, there is, there can only be, the prison and the scourge, or to be cast out in the wilderness to starve.

Consider what it would mean to be under a socialist state. Here for example is a worker who is, who says he is, too ill to work. He begs that he may be set free. The grave official, as Mr. Bellamy sees him, looks at the worker's tongue. "My poor fellow," says he, "you are indeed ill. Go and rest yourself under a shady tree while the others are busy with the harvest." So speaks the ideal official dealing with the ideal citizen in the dream life among the angels. But suppose that the worker, being not an angel but a human being, is but a mere hulking, lazy brute who prefers to sham sick rather than endure the tedium of toil. Or suppose that the grave official is not an angel, but a man of hateful heart or one with a personal spite to vent upon his victim. What then? How could one face a régime in which the everlasting taskmaster held control? There is nothing like it among us at the present day except within the melancholy precincts of the penitentiary. There and there only, the socialist system is in operation.

Who can deny that under such a system the man with the glib tongue and the persuasive manner, the babbling talker and the scheming organizer, would secure all the places of power and profit, while patient merit went to the wall?

Or turn from the gray officials to the purple citizens of the soap bubble commonwealth of socialism. All work, we are told, and all receive their remuneration. We must not think of it as money-wages, but, all said and done, an allotted share of goods, marked out upon a card, comes pretty much to the same thing. The wages that the citizens receive must either be equal or not equal. That at least is plain logic. Either everybody gets exactly the same wages irrespective of capability and diligence, or else the wages or salaries or whatever one calls them, are graded, so that one receives much and the other little.

Now either of these alternatives spells disaster. If the wages are graded according to capacity, then the grading is done by the everlasting elective officials. They can, and they will, vote themselves and their friends or adherents into the good jobs and the high places. The advancement of a bright and capable young man will depend, not upon what he does, but upon what the elected bosses are pleased to do with him; not upon the strength of his own hands, but upon the strength of the "pull" that he has with the bosses who run the part of the industry that he is in. Unequal wages under socialism would mean a fierce and corrupt scramble for power, office and emolument, be-

side which the utmost aberrations of Tammany
Hall would seem as innocuous as a Sunday
School picnic.

"But," objects Mr. Bellamy or any other
socialist, "you forget. Please remember that
under socialism the scramble for wealth is
limited; no man can own capital, but only consumption goods. The most that any man may
acquire is merely the articles that he wants to
consume, not the engines and machinery of production itself. Hence even avarice dwindles
and dies, when its wonted food of 'capitalism'
is withdrawn."

But surely this point of view is the very converse of the teachings of common sense. "Consumption goods" are the very things that we
*do* want. All else is but a means to them.
One admits, as per exception, the queer acquis-
itiveness of the miser-millionaire, playing the
game for his own sake. Undoubtedly he ex-
ists. Undoubtedly his existence is a product of
the system, a pathological product, a kind of
elephantiasis of individualism. But speaking
broadly, consumption goods, present or future,

are the end in sight of the industrial struggle. Give me the houses and the gardens, the yachts, the motor cars and the champagne and I do not care who owns the gravel crusher and the steam plow. And if under a socialist commonwealth a man can vote to himself or gain by the votes of his adherents, a vast income of consumption goods and leave to his unhappy fellow a narrow minimum of subsistence, then the resulting evil of inequality is worse, far worse than it could even be to-day.

Or try, if one will, the other horn of the dilemma. That, too, one will find as ill a resting place as an upright thistle. Let the wages, —as with Mr. Bellamy,—all be equal. The managers then cannot vote themselves large emoluments if they try. But what about the purple citizens? Will they work, or will they lie round in their purple garments and loaf? Work? Why should they work, their pay is there "fresh and fresh"? Why should they turn up on time for their task? Why should they not dawdle at their labor sitting upon the fence in endless colloquy while the harvest rots upon the stalk? If among them is one who cares to work with a fever of industry that even socialism cannot calm, let him do it. We, his fellows, will take our time. Our pay is there as certain and as sound as his. Not for us the eager industry and the fond plans for the future,—for the home and competence—that spurred on the strenuous youth of old days,— not for us the earnest planning of the husband and wife thoughtful and anxious for the future of their little ones. Not for us the honest penny saved for a rainy day. Here in the dreamland of socialism there are no rainy days. It is sunshine all the time in this lotus land of the loafer. And for the future, let the "State" provide; for the children's welfare let the "State" take thought; while we live it shall feed us, when we fall ill it shall tend us and when we die it shall bury us. Meantime let us eat, drink and be merry and work as little as we may. Let us sit among the flowers. It is too hot to labor. Let us warm ourselves beside the public stove. It is too cold to work.

But what? Such conduct, you say, will not

be allowed in the commonwealth. Idleness and slovenly, careless work will be forbidden? Ah! then you must mean that beside the worker will be the overseer with the whip; the time-clock will mark his energy upon its dial; the machine will register his effort; and if he will not work there is lurking for him in the background the shadowed door of the prison. Exactly and logically so. Socialism, in other words, is slavery.

But here the socialist and his school interpose at once with an objection. Under the socialist commonwealth, they say, the people will want to work; they will have acquired a new civic spirit; they will work eagerly and cheerfully for the sake of the public good and from their love of the system under which they live. The loafer will be extinct. The sponge and the parasite will have perished. Even crime itself, so the socialist tells us, will diminish to the vanishing point, till there is nothing of it except here and there a sort of pathological survival, an atavism, or a "throwing back" to the forgotten sins of the grandfathers.

Here and there, some poor fellow afflicted with this disease may break into my socialistic house and steal my pictures and my wine. Poor chap! Deal with him very gently. He is not wicked. He is ill.

This last argument, in a word, begs the whole question. With perfect citizens any government is good. In a population of angels a socialistic commonwealth would work to perfection. But until we have the angels we must keep the commonwealth waiting.

Nor is it necessary here to discuss the hundred and one modifications of the socialistic plan. Each and all fail for one and the same reason. The municipal socialist, despairing of the huge collective state, dreams of his little town as an organic unit in which all share alike; the syndicalist in his fancy sees his trade united into a co-operative body in which all are equal; the gradualist, in whose mind lingers the leaven of doubt, frames for himself a hazy vision of a prolonged preparation for the future, of socialism achieved little by little, the citizens being trained as it goes on till they are to reach somehow or somewhere in cloud land the nirvana of the elimination of self; like indeed, they are, to the horse in the ancient fable that was being trained to live without food but died, alas, just as the experiment was succeeding.

There is no way out. Socialism is but a dream, a bubble floating in the air. In the light of its opalescent colors we may see many visions of what we might be if we were better than we are, we may learn much that is useful as to what we can be even as we are; but if we mistake the floating bubble for the marble palaces of the city of desire, it will lead us forward in our pursuit till we fall over the edge of the abyss beyond which is chaos.

## VII.—What Is Possible and What Is Not

SOCIALISM, then, will not work, and neither will individualism, or at least the older individualism that we have hitherto made the basis of the social order. Here, therefore, stands humanity, in the middle of its narrow path in sheer perplexity, not knowing which way to turn. On either side is the brink of an abyss. On one hand is the yawning gulf of social catastrophe represented by socialism. On the other, the slower, but no less inevitable disaster that would attend the continuation in its present form of the system under which we have lived. Either way lies destruction; the one swift and immediate as a fall from a great height; the other gradual, but equally dreadful, as the slow strangulation in a morass. Somewhere between the two lies such narrow safety as may be found.

The Ancients were fond of the metaphor, taken from the vexed Sicilian Seas, of Scylla and Charybdis. The twin whirlpools threatened the affrighted mariner on either side. To avoid one he too hastily cast the ship to destruction in the other. Such is precisely the position that has been reached at the present crisis in the course of human progress. When we view the shortcomings of the present individualism, its waste of energy, its fretful overwork, its cruel inequality and the bitter lot that it brings to the uncounted millions of the submerged, we are inclined to cry out against it, and to listen with a ready ear to the easy promises of the idealist. But when we turn to the contrasted fallacies of socialism, its obvious impracticality and the dark gulf of social chaos that yawns behind it, we are driven back shuddering to cherish rather the ills we have than fly to others we know not of.

Yet out of the whole discussion of the matter some few things begin to merge into the clearness of certain day. It is clear enough on the one hand that we can expect no sudden and complete transformation of the world in which we live. Such a process is impossible. The industrial system is too complex, its roots are too deeply struck and its whole organism of too delicate a growth to permit us to tear it from the soil. Nor is humanity itself fitted for the kind of transformation which fills the dreams of the perfectionist. The principle of selfishness that has been the survival instinct of existence since life first crawled from the slime of a world in evolution, is as yet but little mitigated. In the long process of time some higher cosmic sense may take its place. It has not done so yet. If the kingdom of socialism were opened to-morrow, there are but few fitted to enter.

But on the other hand it is equally clear that the doctrine of "every man for himself," as it used to be applied, is done with forever. The time has gone by when a man shall starve asking in vain for work; when the listless outcast shall draw his rags shivering about him unheeded of his fellows; when children shall be born in hunger and bred in want and broken in toil with never a chance in life. If nothing else will end these things, fear will do it. The hardest capitalist that ever gripped his property with the iron clasp of legal right relaxes his grasp a little when he thinks of the possibilities of a social conflagration. In this respect five years of war have taught us more than a century of peace. It has set in a clear light new forms of social obligation. The war brought with it conscription—not as we used to see it, as the last horror of military tyranny, but as the crowning pride of democracy. An inconceivable revolution in the thought of the English speaking peoples has taken place in respect to it. The obligation of every man, according to his age and circumstance, to take up arms for his country and, if need be, to die for it, is henceforth the recognized basis of progressive democracy.

But conscription has its other side. The obligation to die must carry with it the right to live. If every citizen owes it to society that he must fight for it in case of need, then society owes to every citizen the opportunity of

a livelihood. "Unemployment," in the case of
the willing and able becomes henceforth a social crime. Every democratic Government
must henceforth take as the starting point of
its industrial policy, that there shall be no such
thing as able bodied men and women "out of
work," looking for occupation and unable to
find it. Work must either be found or must
be provided by the State itself.

Yet it is clear that a policy of state work
and state pay for all who are otherwise unable
to find occupation involves appalling difficulties.
The opportunity will loom large for the prodi-
gal waste of money, for the undertaking of
public works of no real utility and for the sub-
sidizing of an army of loafers. But the difficulties, great though they are, are not insuperable. The payment for state labor of
this kind can be kept low enough to make it
the last resort rather than the ultimate am-
bition of the worker. Nor need the work be
useless. In new countries, especially such as
Canada and the United States and Australia,
the development of latent natural assets could

absorb the labor of generations. There are still unredeemed empires in the west. Clearly enough a certain modicum of public honesty and integrity is essential for such a task; more, undoubtedly, than we have hitherto been able to enlist in the service of the commonwealth. But without it we perish. Social betterment must depend at every stage on the force of public spirit and public morality that inspires it.

So much for the case of those who are able and willing to work. There remain still the uncounted thousands who by accident or illness, age or infirmity, are unable to maintain themselves. For these people, under the older dispensation, there was nothing but the poorhouse, the jail or starvation by the roadside. The narrow individualism of the nineteenth century refused to recognize the social duty of supporting somebody else's grandmother. Such charity began, and ended, at home. But even with the passing of the nineteenth century an awakened sense of the collective responsibility of society towards its weaker members began to impress itself upon public policy.

Old age pension laws and national insurance against illness and accident were already being built into the legislative codes of the democratic countries. The experience of the war has enormously increased this sense of social solidarity. It is clear now that our fortunes are not in our individual keeping. We stand or fall as a nation. And the nation which neglects the aged and infirm, or which leaves a family to be shipwrecked as the result of a single accident to a breadwinner, cannot survive as against a nation in which the welfare of each is regarded as contributory to the safety of all. Even the purest selfishness would dictate a policy of social insurance.

There is no need to discuss the particular way in which this policy can best be carried out. It will vary with the circumstances of each community. The action of the municipality, or of the state or province, or of the central government itself may be called into play. But in one form or another, the economic loss involved in illness and infirmity must be shifted from the shoulders of the individual to those of society at large. There was but little realization of this obligation in the nineteenth century. Only in the sensational moments of famine, flood or pestilence was a general social effort called forth. But in the clearer view of the social bond which the war has given us we can see that famine and pestilence are merely exaggerated forms of what is happening every day in our midst.

We spoke much during the war of "man power." We suddenly realized that after all the greatness and strength of a nation is made up of the men and women who compose it. Its money, in the narrow sense, is nothing; a set of meaningless chips and counters piled upon a banker's table ready to fall at a touch. Even before the war we had begun to talk eagerly and anxiously of the conservation of national resources, of the need of safeguarding the forests and fisheries and the mines. These are important things. But the war has shown that the most important thing of all is the conservation of men and women.

The attitude of the nineteenth century upon

this point was little short of insane. The melancholy doctrine of Malthus had perverted the public mind. Because it was difficult for a poor man to bring up a family, the hasty conclusion was reached that a family ought not to be brought up. But the war has entirely inverted and corrected this point of view. The father and mother who were able to send six sturdy, native-born sons to the conflict were regarded as benefactors of the nation. But these six sturdy sons had been, some twenty years before, six "puling infants," viewed with gloomy disapproval by the Malthusian bachelor. If the strength of the nation lies in its men and women there is only one way to increase it. Before the war it was thought that a simpler and easier method of increase could be found in the wholesale import of Austrians, Bulgarians and Czecho-Slovaks. The newer nations boasted proudly of their immigration tables. The fallacy is apparent now. Those who really count in a nation and those who govern its destinies for good or ill are those who are born in it.

It is difficult to over-estimate the harm that

has been done to public policy by this same
Malthusian theory. It has opposed to every
proposal of social reform an obstacle that
seemed insuperable,—the danger of a rapid
overincrease of population that would pauper-
ize the community. Population, it was said,
tends always to press upon the heels of subsistence. If the poor are pampered, they will
breed fast: the time will come when there will
not be food for all and we shall perish in a
common destruction. Seen in this light, infant
mortality and the cruel wastage of disease were
viewed with complacence. It was "Nature's"
own process at work. The "unfit," so called,
were being winnowed out that only the best
might survive. The biological doctrine of evolution was misinterpreted and misapplied to
social policy.

But in the organic world there is no such
thing as the "fit" or the "unfit," in any higher
or moral sense. The most hideous forms of
life may "survive" and thrust aside the most
beautiful. It is only by a confusion of thought
that the processes of organic nature which ren-

der every foot of fertile ground the scene of
unending conflict can be used to explain away
the death of children of the slums.   The whole
theory of survival is only a statement of what
is, not of what ought to be.   The moment that
we introduce the operation of human volition
and activity, that, too, becomes one of the factors of "survival."   The dog, the cat, and the
cow live by man's will, where the wolf and the
hyena have perished.

But it is time that the Malthusian doctrine,—
the fear of over-population as a hindrance to
social reform,—was dismissed from considera-
tion.   It is at best but a worn-out scarecrow
shaking its vain rags in the wind.   Population,
it is true, increases in a geometrical ratio.   The
human race, if favored by environment, can
easily double itself every twenty-five years.   If
it did this, the time must come, through sheer
power of multiplication, when there would not
be standing room for it on the globe.   All of
this is undeniable, but it is quite wide of the
mark.   It is time enough to cross a bridge when
we come to it.   The "standing room" prob-

lem is still removed from us by such uncounted generations that we need give no thought to it. The physical resources of the globe are as yet only tapped, and not exhausted. We have done little more than scratch the surface. Because we are crowded here and there in the ant-hills of our cities, we dream that the world is full. Because, under our present system, we do not raise enough food for all, we fear that the food supply is running short. All this is pure fancy. Let any one consider in his mind's eye the enormous untouched assets still remaining for mankind in the vast spaces filled with the tangled forests of South America, or the exuberant fertility of equatorial Africa or the huge plains of Canada, Australia, Southern Siberia and the United States, as yet only thinly dotted with human settlement. There is no need to draw up an anxious balance sheet of our assets. There is still an uncounted plenty. And every human being born upon the world represents a power of work that, rightly directed, more than supplies his wants. The fact that as an infant he does not maintain himself has nothing to do with the case. This was true even in the Garden of Eden.

The fundamental error of the Malthusian theory of population and poverty is to confound the difficulties of human organization with the question of physical production. Our existing poverty is purely a problem in the direction and distribution of human effort. It has no connection as yet with the question of the total available means of subsistence. Some day, in a remote future, in which under an improved social system the numbers of mankind might increase to the full power of the natural capacity of multiplication, such a question might conceivably disturb the equanimity of mankind. But it need not now. It is only one of many disasters that must sooner or later overtake mankind. The sun, so the astronomer tells us, is cooling down; the night is coming; an all-pervading cold will some day chill into rigid death the last vestige of organic life. Our poor planet will be but a silent ghost whirling on its dark path in the starlight. This ultimate disaster is, as far as our vision goes, inevitable. Yet no one concerns himself with it. So should it be with the danger of the ultimate overcrowding of the globe.

I lay stress upon this problem of the increase of population because, to my thinking, it is in this connection that the main work and the best hope of social reform can be found. The children of the race should be the very blossom of its fondest hopes. Under the present order and with the present gloomy preconceptions they have been the least of its collective cares. Yet here—and here more than anywhere—is the point towards which social effort and social legislation may be directed immediately and successfully. The moment that we get away from the idea that the child is a mere appendage of the parent, bound to share good fortune and ill, wealth and starvation, according to the parent's lot, the moment we regard the child as itself a member of society—clothed in social rights—a burden for the moment but an asset for the future—we turn over a new leaf in the book of human development, we pass a new milestone on the upward path of progress.

It should be recognized in the coming order of society, that every child of the nation has the right to be clothed and fed and trained irrespective of its parents' lot. Our feeble beginnings in the direction of housing, sanitation, child welfare and education, should be expanded at whatever cost into something truly national and all embracing. The ancient grudging selfishness that would not feed other people's children should be cast out. In the war time the wealthy bachelor and the spinster of advancing years took it for granted that other people's children should fight for them. The obligation must apply both ways.

No society is properly organized until every child that is born into it shall have an opportunity in life. Success in life and capacity to live we cannot give. But opportunity we can. We can at least see that the gifts that are laid in the child's cradle by nature are not obliterated by the cruel fortune of the accident of

birth: that its brain and body are not stunted
by lack of food and air and by the heavy burden of premature toil. The playtime of childhood should be held sacred by the nation.

This, as I see it, should be the first and the
greatest effort of social reform. For the
adult generation of to-day many things are no
longer possible. The time has passed. We
are, as viewed with a comprehensive eye, a
damaged race. Few of us in mind or body are
what we might be; and millions of us, the vast
majority of industrial mankind known as the
working class, are distorted beyond repair from
what they might have been. In older societies
this was taken for granted: the poor and the
humble and the lowly reproduced from generation to generation, as they grew to adult life,
the starved brains and stunted outlook of their
forbears,—starved and stunted only by lack of
opportunity. For nature knows of no such differences in original capacity between the children of the fortunate and the unfortunate.
Yet on this inequality, made by circumstance,
was based the whole system of caste, the strati-

fication of the gentle and the simple on which
society rested. In the past it may have been
necessary. It is not so now. If, with all our
vast apparatus of machinery and power, we
cannot so arrange society that each child has
an opportunity in life, it would be better to
break the machinery in pieces and return to
the woods from which we came.

Put into the plainest of prose, then, we are
saying that the government of every country
ought to supply work and pay for the unemployed, maintenance for the infirm and aged,
and education and opportunity for the children.
These are vast tasks. And they involve, of
course, a financial burden not dreamed of before the war. But here again the war has
taught us many things. It would have seemed
inconceivable before, that a man of great
wealth should give one-half of his income to
the state. The financial burden of the war,
as the full measure of it dawned upon our
minds, seemed to betoken a universal bank-
ruptcy. But the sequel is going to show that
the finance of the war will prove to be a lesson

in the finance of peace. The new burden has come to stay. No modern state can hope to survive unless it meets the kind of social claims on the part of the unemployed, the destitute and the children that have been described above. And it cannot do this unless it continues to use the terrific engine of taxation already fashioned in the war. Undoubtedly the progressive income tax and the tax on profits and taxation of inheritance must be maintained to an extent never dreamed of before.

But the peace finance and the war finance will differ in one most important respect. The war finance was purely destructive. From it came national security and the triumph of right over wrong. No one would belittle the worth of the sacrifice. But in the narrower sense of production, of bread winning, there came nothing; or nothing except a new power of organization, a new technical skill and a new aspiration towards better things. But the burden of peace finance directed towards social efforts will bring a direct return. Every cent that is spent upon the betterment of the population will come back, sooner or later, as two.

But all of this deals as yet only with the field of industry and conduct in which the state rules supreme. Governmental care of the unemployed, the infant and the infirm, sounds like a chapter in socialism. If the same régime were extended over the whole area of production, we should have socialism itself and a mere soap-bubble bursting into fragments. There is no need, however, to extend the régime of compulsion over the whole field. The vast mass of human industrial effort must still lie outside of the immediate control of the government. Every man will still earn his own living and that of his family as best he can, relying first and foremost upon his own efforts.

One naturally asks, then, To what extent can social reform penetrate into the ordinary operation of industry itself? Granted that it is impossible for the state to take over the whole industry of the nation, does that mean that the present inequalities must continue? The framework in which our industrial life is set

cannot be readily broken asunder. But we can
to a great extent ease the rigidity of its out-
lines. A legislative code that starts from
sounder principles than those which have ob-
tained hitherto can do a great deal towards
progressive betterment. Each decade can be
an improvement upon the last. Hitherto we
have been hampered at every turn by the supposed obstacle of immutable economic laws.
The theory of "natural" wages and prices of
a supposed economic order that could not be
disturbed, set up a sort of legislative paralysis.
The first thing needed is to get away entirely
from all such preconceptions, to recognize that
the "natural" order of society, based on the
"natural" liberty, does not correspond with real
justice and real liberty at all, but works injus-
tice at every turn. And at every turn intrusive
social legislation must seek to prevent such in-
justice.

It is no part of the present essay to attempt
to detail the particulars of a code of social legislation. That must depend in every case upon
the particular circumstances of the community

concerned.   But some indication may be given
here of the kind of legislation that may serve
to render the conditions of industry more in
conformity with social justice.   Let us take, as
a conspicuous example, the case of the Minimum wage law.   Here is a thing sternly con-
demned in the older thought as an economic
impossibility.   It was claimed, as we have seen,
that under free contract a man was paid
what he earned and no law could make it more.
But the older theory was wrong.   The minimum wage law ought to form, in one fashion
or another, a part of the code of every community.   It may be applied by specific legislation from a central power, or it may be applied
by the discretionary authority of district boards,
or it may be regulated,—as it has been in some
of the beginnings already made,—within the
compass of each industry or trade.   But the
principle involved is sound.   The wage as paid
becomes a part of the conditions of industry.
Interest, profits and, later, the direction of consumption and then of production, conform
themselves to it.

True it is, that in this as in all cases of social legislation, no application of the law can be made so sweeping and so immediate as to dislocate the machine and bring industry to a stop. It is probable that at any particular time and place the legislative minimum wage cannot be very much in advance of the ordinary or average wage of the people in employment. But its virtue lies in its progression. The modest increase of to-day leads to the fuller increase of to-morrow. Properly applied, the capitalist and the employer of labor need have nothing to fear from it. Its ultimate effect will not fall upon them, but will serve merely to alter the direction of human effort.

Precisely the same reasoning holds good of the shortening of the hours of labor both by legislative enactment and by collective organization. Here again the first thing necessary is a clear vision of the goal towards which we are to strive. The hours of labor are too long. The world has been caught in the wheels of its own machinery which will not stop. With each advance in invention and mechanical power it

works harder still. New and feverish desires
for luxuries replace each older want as satisfied.
The nerves of our industrial civilization are
worn thin with the rattle of its own machinery.
The industrial world is restless, over-strained
and quarrelsome. It seethes with furious discontent, and looks about it eagerly for a fight.
It needs a rest. It should be sent, as nerve
patients are, to the seaside or the quiet of the
hills. Failing this, it should at least slacken
the pace of its work and shorten its working
day.

And for this the thing needed is an altered
public opinion on the subject of work in relation to human character and development.
The nineteenth century glorified work. The
poet, sitting beneath a shady tree, sang of its
glories. The working man was incited to con-
template the beauty of the night's rest that followed on the exhaustion of the day. It was
proved to him that if his day was dull at least
his sleep was sound. The ideal of society was
the cheery artisan and the honest blacksmith,
awake and singing with the lark and busy all

day long at the loom and the anvil, till the grateful night soothed them into well-earned slumber. This, they were told, was better than the distracted sleep of princes.

The educated world repeated to itself these grotesque fallacies till it lost sight of plain and simple truths. Seven o'clock in the morning is too early for any rational human being to be herded into a factory at the call of a steam whistle. Ten hours a day of mechanical task is too long: nine hours is too long: eight hours is too long. I am not raising here the question as to how and to what extent the eight hours can be shortened, but only urging the primary need of recognizing that a working day of eight hours is too long for the full and proper development of human capacity and for the rational enjoyment of life. There is no need to quote here to the contrary the long and sustained toil of the pioneer, the eager labor of the student, unmindful of the silent hours, or the fierce acquisitive activity of the money-maker that knows no pause. Activities such as these differ with a whole sky from the wage-work of the modern industrial worker. The task in one case is done for its own sake. It is life itself. The other is done only for the sake of the wage it brings. It is, or should be, a mere preliminary to living.

Let it be granted, of course, that a certain amount of work is an absolute necessity for human character. There is no more pathetic spectacle on our human stage than the figure of poor puppy in his beach suit and his tuxedo jacket seeking in vain to amuse himself for ever. A leisure class no sooner arises than the melancholy monotony of amusement forces it into mimic work and make-believe activities. It dare not face the empty day.

But when all is said about the horror of idleness the broad fact remains that the hours of work are too long. If we could in imagination disregard for a moment all question of how the hours of work are to be shortened and how production is to be maintained and ask only what would be the ideal number of the daily hours of compulsory work, for character's sake, few of us would put them at more

than four or five. Many of us, as applied to
ourselves, at least, would take a chance on character at two.

The shortening of the general hours of work,
then, should be among the primary aims of
social reform. There need be no fear that
with shortened hours of labor the sum total of
production would fall short of human needs.
This, as has been shown from beginning to end
of this essay, is out of the question. Human
*desires* would eat up the result of ten times the
work we now accomplish. Human *needs*
would be satisfied with a fraction of it. But
the real difficulty in the shortening of hours lies
elsewhere. Here, as in the parallel case of the
minimum wage, the danger is that the attempt
to alter things too rapidly may dislocate the industrial machine. We ought to attempt such
a shortening as will strain the machine to a
breaking point, but never break it. This can
be done, as with the minimum wage, partly by
positive legislation and partly collective action.
Not much can be done at once. But the process can be continuous. The short hours

achieved with acclamation to-day will later be
denounced as the long hours of to-morrow.
The essential point to grasp, however, is that
society at large has nothing to lose by the
process. The shortened hours become a part
of the framework of production. It adapts itself to it. Hitherto we have been caught in
the running of our own machine: it is time that
we altered the gearing of it.

The two cases selected,—the minimum wage
and the legislative shortening of hours,—have
been chosen merely as illustrations and are not
exhaustive of the things that can be done in the
field of possible and practical reform. It is
plain enough that in many other directions the
same principles may be applied. The rectifica-
tion of the ownership of land so as to eliminate
the haphazard gains of the speculator and the
unearned increment of wealth created by the
efforts of others, is an obvious case in point.
The "single taxer" sees in this a cure-all for
the ills of society. But his vision is distorted.
The private ownership of land is one of the
greatest incentives to human effort that the

world has ever known. It would be folly to abolish it, even if we could. But here as elsewhere we can seek to re-define and regulate the conditions of ownership so as to bring them more into keeping with a common sense view of social justice.

But the inordinate and fortuitous gains from land are really only one example from a general class. The war discovered the "profiteer." The law-makers of the world are busy now with smoking him out from his lair. But he was there all the time. Inordinate and fortuitous gain, resting on such things as monopoly, or trickery, or the mere hazards of abundance and scarcity, complying with the letter of the law but violating its spirit, are fit objects for appropriate taxation. The ways and means are difficult, but the social principle involved is clear.

We may thus form some sort of vision of the social future into which we are passing. The details are indistinct. But the outline at least in which it is framed is clear enough. The safety of the future lies in a progressive movement of social control alleviating the misery which it cannot obliterate and based upon the broad general principle of equality of opportunity. The chief immediate direction of social effort should be towards the attempt to give to every human being in childhood adequate food, clothing, education and an opportunity in life. This will prove to be the beginning of many things.

THE END